THREE IRON M   TOWNS

A Study in Cultural Change

THREE IRON MINING TOWNS
A Study in Cultural Change

by

PAUL H. LANDIS

Associate Professor of Sociology
The State College of Washington
now
Washington State University

with a new foreword
by
William R Freudenburg & Robert Gramling

Social Ecology Press
P.O. Box 620863
Middleton, WI 53562-0863
1997

Publisher's Cataloging-in-Publication
(Provided by Quality Books, Inc.)

Landis, Paul Henry, 1901-1985
    Three iron mining towns : a study in cultural
change / Paul H. Landis.   --2nd ed.
    p. cm. --(Classic studies in rural sociology.)
    ISBN: 0-941042-19-7

    1. Iron mines and mining--Minnesota--St. Louis
County. 2. Human ecology--Minnesota--St. Louis
County. 3. Mesabi Range (Minn.) 4. Eveleth (Minn.)
5. Hibbing (Minn.) 6. Virginia (Minn.) I. Title.

F612.M36L32 1997   304.2'09776'77
                          QB197-40664

Second edition paperback published 1997
by Social Ecology Press

Social Ecology Press ™
P.O. Box 620863
Middleton, WI 53562-0863

Printed in the United States of America on recycled paper

10 9 8 7 6 5 4 3 2 1

Foreword

With the republication of the Paul Landis classic, Three Mining Towns, a new generation of community scholars will be able to enjoy the kind of ready access to this fine work that is best permitted by being able to have a copy on one's own bookshelf. What these new readers are likely to learn is that Paul Landis' sweeping analysis of an important set of resource-dependent communities is like a proverbial breath of fresh air.

Given that the work was originally published in 1938, it is in some ways representative of that time. It shows considerable faith in technological growth, for example, despite the effects of the Great Depression. In addition, small linguistic markers, such as what many of today's readers will find to be a quaint handling of issues such as prostitution and ethnic origin, provide occasional reminders that this is a historical document. Overall, however, what stands out is a combination of characteristics that is remarkable even today: exceptional care in the selection of the case study communities, coupled with the conceptual courage to consider the changes in these communities at a much broader level of analysis.

In many small ways, the book presages "discoveries" that occurred much later in the discipline, but there are three major aspects of the book that are likely to prove particularly instructive for those who will be encountering the work today, more that six decades after it was first written. First, even though the first three of those decades were to be ones which the connections between humans and their environments would often be carefully overlooked, Landis consistently and quite naturally examines the relationship between human activities and the physical environment. Throughout the volume, he reminds us that factors such as the richness of nearby iron ore or forest resources can strongly affect human communities-and that human activities such as the rate of extraction, whether of iron ore or trees, will affect both the environment and its capacity to support subsequent human endeavors. One of the benefits of being able to read Landis' work today, in fact, is that his consideration of these variables is so integral to his analysis as to remind us that it was not necessary for the discipline to have lost sight of them, and that it should not have needed to be such an uphill fight when environmental sociology began to emerge as a self-conscious specialty in the 1970s.

The second major theme-as indicated by but also going well beyond the implications of the title-is that the analysis is comparative. Another present-day rediscovery is that, if we want to examine environmental and technological variables, we need to design our research so that these environmental and technological variables can vary. This is not just a matter of scale: whenever the focus is on a single entity, whether at the level of rural community or of an entire global system of economic or political power, the abilities to make comparisons across and to note variations across "cases" is inherently constricted. The case study is a wonderful tool, and certainly the two of us have done case studies ourselves, but the danger of this tool is that, since a number of important variables are effectively held constant for any given case, those variables can quickly disappear from sight, becoming "naturalized" or being taken for granted, escaping the analyst's attention. Landis apparently understood this important risk. His book is explicitly comparative throughout, not just in the sense of comparing the three towns to one another, but also through any number of comparisons of mining dependence against other key ways in which rural communities have supported themselves-ranging from a dependence on logging, which had characterized the region in earlier years, to the potential dependence on agriculture or tourism that seemed to hold at least some potential as future options at the time.

Finally, the book is well written. Landis strings words and ideas together in a clear, direct, jargon-free style that is easy to read and understand. This is probably not the place for extensive commentary on the proliferation of jargon in sociology, nor for arguing whether the end result of that process has been for the better or worse. Neither of us had even been born in 1938, let alone begun to study sociology at that time. It is worth noting, however, that the English language provides rich resources for communication. Landis' use of it reminds us that in cases where the language may appear to be incapable of communication an idea, it may indicate a linguistic shortcoming-but it may also indicate a lack of clarity in the first place.

In sum, Social Ecology Press has made a wise decision with their publication of Three Iron Mining Towns. This classic study is a refreshing reminder of our past. It will help the thoughtful reader to realize that, while we have come a long way since 1938 in terms of our methodological sophistication, we may have forgotten some important basics along the way. By re-reading this classic today, we have an opportunity to do better in the future, based in part on a better understanding of this rich legacy from our past.

William R. Freudenburg

Robert Gramling

PREFACE

The frontier and especially the mining town has often been made the setting for American fiction, no doubt primarily because frontier life has color. Human nature appears in the rough for there is no time for the embellishments which come to mask it in more stable environments.

The frontier is no less a suitable subject for the student of sociology. He, also, is interested in personality and in the social processes that operate on the frontier where life is less controlled by long-established custom and law.

This study is interested in personalities and in groups as influences in setting social processes in motion and in producing changes in culture. It is concerned fundamentally with an analysis of the shifting social interaction patterns which characterize a community as its group composition is modified during its normal growth to maturity and in showing how persistent interaction patterns determine the trend of cultural growth during its life cycle.

Few industries that establish community life are more short lived than mining. The short life cycle offers an unusual opportunity to bring the historical processes of social and cultural change of a community within the scope of a special study. The short span of time involved permits an accurate observation of the incidence of change; the speed of development permits observation of the processes of growth and maturity; the homogeneity of the economic and industrial base permits an observation little complicated by a multiplicity of distinct social classes and social standards. Under such circumstances one can be fairly sure of what is going on and why. Even though the study deals with a single area, the processes and relationships revealed no doubt characterize a larger universe.

Acknowledgment is made to the <u>American Journal of Sociology</u> (University of Chicago Press); <u>Social Forces</u> (University of North Carolina Press); and to <u>Economic Geography</u> (Clark University) for permission to reproduce materials originally published in these journals.

Pullman, Washington
January 2, 1938

TABLE OF CONTENTS

Chapter   Page

PART I--FACTORS IN CULTURE BUILDING

I   Introduction.. 3
      The Mesabi Iron Range and Its Town........ 3
      Field of Study.. 5
      Assumptions and Hypotheses..................... 7
      Use of Terms... 8

II   The Geographical Factor in Range History......... 10
      Resources of the Mesabi........................... 10
      Early Uses of the Mesabi.......................... 11
      Discovery of Mesabi Ore........................... 12
      The Mesabi in an Iron Age......................... 13
      Location in Relation to Industry...................15
      The Utilization of Other Resources
           in the Environment....................... 16
      Summary...................................... 17

III   Population in Relation to Cultural Adjustment.... 18
      The Population Perspective....................... 18
      Phenomenal Growth of Range Towns........ 19
      Disproportionate Number of Males........... 19
      Birth and Death Rates Gradually
           Approach Normal......................... 20
      Excess of Violent Deaths........................... 20
      Suicides....................................... 21
      Immigrant Population.............................. 22
      Conclusion.................................... 24

TABLE OF CONTENTS

Chapter   Page

PART II--GROUP ADJUSTMENTS DURING THE
HISTORY OF THE RANGE

IV   The Pioneer Period.................................... 27
      The Transition from Pioneer Society......... 32

V   The Period of Conflict............................... 36
      Hibbing Defies the Mining Companies.... 37
      Hibbing Submits to Mining Companies... 41
      Eveleth Buys a Reputation Through
      Athletic Achievements........................... 42
      Virginia Capitalized Prosperity............... 45

VI   The Period of Struggle for Survival...................... 47
      Building a Trade Hinterland..................... 48
      Baiting a Tourist Trade............................ 51
      The Leach Town... 51
      How Long Will Ore Last?........................... 53

PART III--CULTURAL CHANGE
IN THE MESABI TOWNS

A. Pioneer Folkways and Mores

VII   The Realistic Nature of Pioneer Folkways........... 57
      Food.. 57
      Industry... 57
      Merchandising.. 58
      Shelter.. 59
      Sex Satisfaction....................................... 59
      Relaxation.. 60

Chapter		Page
VIII	The Tolerant Nature of Pioneer Mores	62
	Respectability of Saloon Keeper and Saloon	62
	Accepted Behavior	63
	Tolerance of Illegal Enterprises	65
	Low Evaluation of Life	66
	Protection	68
	Religion	68
	Democracy	68
	Shaking Off Pioneer Mores	69
	B. Culture Building during the Period of Extravagance	
IX	Community Gratification Through Public Services	71
	Public Utilities	71
	Education	72
	Municipal Recreation Facilities	75
X	Perversions in Spending	78
	Differential Spending	82
XI	The Evolution of the Ore Taxation Policy	86
	Participation of Range Towns in Taxation Developments	86
	Increasing Municipal Valuations by the Annexation of Ore Properties	89
	The Evolution of State Taxation Policy	90
	An Analysis of the Factors in Evolution of Ore Taxation Policy	91
XII	The Development of Political Mores	94
	What Are the Political Mores?	94

Chapter		Page

Factors in the Development of the
Political Mores.............................. 98
    Summary.. 104

XIII Lags in Group Adjustment.............................. 105
    Regions of Strain in Mining Company
        Labor Relations--The Machine--
        Strikes--Unemployment............. 105

Public Sympathy with Labor............................ 110
    Community Spending, the Region of
        Strain in Public-Mining Company
        Relations...................................... 110

PART IV--AN ANALYSIS OF CULTURAL CHANGE

XIV The Role of the Great Man in Culture Change..... 114

XV The Life Cycle of the Iron Mining Town.............. 117
    Physico-Social Cycles............................... 117
    Bio-Social Cycles...................................... 119
    Psycho-Social Cycles.............................. 124
    Cultural Cycles...................................... 128
    Summary.. 130

XVI Where Does the Dynamics of Cultural
    Change Reside?...................................... 138
    Cultural Change and Social Change
        as Distinct Processes................. 138
    Relation of Group Interaction Pattern
        to the Culture Pattern............... 139
    Culture Change as the Product of
        Interaction...................................... 141

PART I

FACTORS IN CULTURE BUILDING

Chapter I[1]

INTRODUCTION

The Mesabi Iron Range and Its Towns

Driving northward in Minnesota some two hundred miles above the Twin Cities, one reaches a wilderness of burned-over stumps, second-growth evergreens, tamarack, and underbrush scattered over rocky hills intervened by swampy valleys or crystal lakes. An occasional farmhouse suggests the presence of human life. The area bespeaks an age of timber now past some thirty years, and an agriculture as yet unborn. The charred stumps and deadened trees indicate the passing of devastating fires. The highway at a distance of some sixty miles north of Duluth leads into cities located in the most unsuspected places--cities blotted on the rugged surface features of an iron range.

This iron-bearing district is known as the Mesabi[2] Range. Some sixty miles inland from the northwestern end of Lake Superior it extends for a distance of approximately eighty miles toward the southwest. Here a narrow strip of hills marks the zone of the world's largest iron ore mines, the mines that have fed the manufacturing cities of the lower lake states for a generation, and will continue to feed them for perhaps another generation.

In the lapse of a few years the ore discoveries of the Mesabi shifted the iron and steel trade from the Ohio valley to the Great Lakes, built eight railroads, caused the development of more than twenty flourishing towns, placed on the Great Lakes the largest commercial fleet in the world, and gave America world supremacy in the iron and steel industry.

The Mesabi cities have sprung up comparable in many respects to those in other areas of American culture. Immigrants have come to these cities from many nations to mine ore, rear families, and become citizens. Three of the most successful municipalities have been chosen for study. Hibbing has a population of about 16,000 at the present time. She is a village by her own choice, for some thirty-five years ago she might have been incorporated as a city. She is the wealthy village that boasts of a taxable valuation of $93,000,000 and which has for years spent approximately $2,000,000 in tax moneys annually--a village that is self-labeled "The Iron Ore Capital of the World."

Virginia, the "Queen City of the Range," is the second municipality chosen for study. Virginia boasts of 12,000 population now, though at one time she possessed 2000 more. This city has the "world's largest white pine mill" (now idle), and is also the center of valuable mines and fine public works. It has a national reputation for the successful operation of municipal utilities--its heat, electricity, water, and sewerage systems are unrivaled by any American community. Here history is colored with catastrophe, fires at two different periods having almost completely reduced the city to ashes.

Eveleth, the third city, has a population of 7500. It is also a mining town, is the most foreign in population, and, at the present time, is more frequently accused of graft than any other range town. Eveleth is the "City on the Hill" by her own designation. At one time she gained a national reputation for athletics, which led to an aftermath of lawsuits involving indictments for the illegal use of city funds.

Hibbing is located at the west end of the Range; Virginia and Eveleth are some thirty-five miles eastward in the center of the Range and are only four miles apart. All three municipalities, and most of the Mesabi Range, are in St. Louis County, Minnesota.

The Virginia town site was originally platted between Silver and Virginia Lakes, and on September 16, 1892, the first lots were sold. On December 7 of the same-year the first train arrived over the Duluth Mesabi and

Northern, carrying those interested in business and home-making.

Hibbing had its humble beginning in 1893. Hibbing and Trimble, partners in exploration, located the town site in the midst of a great pine forest. A clearing was begun June 11, and lots were plotted and sold.

The village of Eveleth was founded in 1893 by two explorers, the most active of the two being David T. Adams. He named the town for a timber cruiser in the district. "Hank Hookwith came in to open a saloon. Archie McComb had a hotel building (afterwards destroyed by fire), and Jerry Sullivan had a boarding house on the side of the future town...." [3]

In such a manner the Mesabi towns that provide the subject matter for this study were born. Today they are the chief municipalities of the Mesabi.

Field of Study

The Mesabi Iron Range presents an opportunity for a study of change that is in many respects ideal. The Range was discovered after the development of the modern newspaper, so that during the early history of each town studied, a newspaper was published and consecutive copies for most years have been filed in the library of the State Historical Society.[4] Machine technique, too was well developed, as were modern means of transportation. The demand for iron ore was at its height soon after the discovery of the Range, and the newly-formed United States Steel Corporation and other great capitalistic interests bought up most of the important ore reserves. These combined factors have hastened change in the modifiable characteristics of the natural environment and in the rate of development of culture in a way that has scarcely been equaled elsewhere. Wave after wave of settlers came to the Mesabi for the

rewards of work--wages, merchandising profits, and
professional salaries. This latter situation offers a possibility for studying the effects of the changing complexion of
groups on culture. On the Mesabi, then, one has a fast
moving panorama of change. The interactions of changing
social groups in a rapidly changing environment have
combined with a rapid rate of cultural change. The whole
drama has been played in forty years.

The exploitation of America's natural resources has
led to the establishment of many one-industry towns. Some
of these towns have been built by the companies exploiting
the natural resource and have been completely controlled
by them. In other towns the industrial concern has developed the resource only, leaving the matter of town development entirely to the public that gathered around the infant
industry. The Mesabi Iron Range communities are of the
latter type. The iron mining companies obtained the underground rights only, being interested primarily in iron ore.
The surface rights belonged to the public and were controlled by them. The Mesabi towns, which are the subject of
this study, are not, then, company towns. Company towns
are usually subject to the complete domination and control
of the industry. The Mesabi towns are independent. This
must be kept in mind if the vivid drama of public-mining-
company conflict that has characterized the socio-economic
and political patterns of the Mesabi towns is to be fully
appreciated.

The study is an analysis of one of many phases of
American frontier life. It traces a primitive mining settlement through its founding, youth and maturity. The mining
settlement is but one of many phases of the American
frontier, but none the less possesses many characteristics
which are indicative of the patterns of life as they existed
a few years ago in many parts of the nation. The Mesabi
frontier, like most of the frontiers, is now a matter of
history and reminiscence, for the community has reached
maturity and is approaching old age.

This study gives a close-up picture of the clash of class interests as they have existed in American industrial experience. It also shows the American melting pot in ferment, as thousands of raw immigrants from all the European countries were molded, first into the industrial patterns of the range and then into the social and political completion of the community.

Assumptions and Hypotheses

The basic questions to be answered with regard to the nature of cultural change in the mining town insofar as this study is concerned are:

1. Does cultural change in the mining town occur according to some pattern that can be fairly accurately described?

2. If some pattern of change is present, how is it to be accounted for? If none exists, then why is culture subject to no observable sequences such as are found in other levels of phenomena?

Since it is assumed that cultural dynamics does not necessarily reside in the culture itself, it is legitimate to seek for causes of cultural change outside of culture. We may seek the drive for cultural change in the social group or in its habitat, as well as in the history of the culture.

In accordance with this position the following hypotheses are postulated:
1. Cultural change in the mining town probably occurs according to a pattern that can be observed and described.
2. If the first hypothesis is correct, the forces determining the pattern of change can perhaps be located in culture itself or in these closely related realms of phenomena which are intimately connected with culture--the world of human qualities or of natural conditions.

3. The most fruitful place to seek the forces determining cultural change is in the social group.

More specific statements of hypotheses are made in connection with the data presented in different sections of the study.

The approach in this study is, then, synthetic in the sense that various levels of phenomena are considered as possible sources of energy causing cultural change. Particular attention is given to the bearing of group interaction upon cultural change, although the effects of cultural history, of geographical factors and of biological factors are considered.

Use of Terms

Culture: Civilization. The term is used in its anthropological sense to include both material and non-material traits.

Society: Interacting groups inhabiting a common area. In this case the iron range towns are the area, and the groups are the industrial and labor groups and the public.

Industrial group: Managers and owners of the iron mining industry.

Labor group: Chiefly the laborers in the iron mining industry.

Public: Those who are neither mine laborers nor industrialists, but who, as members of the community, are necessarily concerned in the activities of the other two groups. The public consists largely of professional men, business men, and technicians.

Interaction: A blanket term covering the various processes of inter-group and intra-group intercourse, such as conflict, cooperation, domination, and subordination.

Community, town, municipality: All of these terms are used interchangeably in referring to the towns studied. A rigid distinction between village, town, and city is difficult to follow since two of the municipalities have passed through the first two of these stages and are now cities, while Hibbing has always remained a village even though it is the largest of all Mesabi Range municipalities.

Footnotes for chapter I

1. This publication is a digest of the observations and conclusions of a doctor's dissertation on Three Mesabi Iron Range Towns. Substantiating evidence, documentary citations, and interview summaries are for the most part omitted here for the sake of brevity. Bound copies of the full manuscript, including a bibliography of 180 titles, are on file in the Library of the University of Minnesota and in the Department of Sociology there. For the most part names of persons are fictitious although each name represents a real character on the Mesabi Iron Range.

2. "Mesabi" is the spelling accepted by the National Association of Geographers. This is the form used throughout this work except where the name has another spelling in the names of railroad companies, etc.

3. Van Brunt, Walter, History of Duluth and St. Louis County, ch. 22.

4. The Hibbing Sentinel: The Virginia Enterprise: The Eveleth Mining New.

Chapter II

THE GEOGRAPHICAL FACTOR IN RANGE HISTORY

It is difficult to strip a geographical area of its cultural super-structure in order to see it in its purely natural aspects. Once culture building begins, the setting may be radically changed, especially where the culture building group is possessed of technological devices capable of controlling nature to a considerable degree.

A survey of the history of the people who have inhabited the Mesabi indicates that different groups have utilized different natural resources. For instance, one group has sought wild game, another tillable soil, another minerals. The natural environment has been relatively constant for several centuries. Consequently, all present resources have been available to previous groups. Yet, each group has specialized in exploiting a selected resource. This fact merits an explanation.

Resources of the Mesabi

From our present knowledge, it appears that the original resources of the Mesabi Range were: (1) <u>Flora</u>, a virgin forest, principally pine; undergrowth with fruits and berries in great abundance; pin cherries, choke cherries, June berries, raspberries, strawberries, huckleberries, and blueberries; (2) <u>Fauna</u>, moose; bear and deer; many small game animals and furbearing animals; waterfowl and freshwater fish abounding in the lakes; (3) <u>Soil</u>, a fertile and well-watered soil, but rugged and rocky, in places swampy, and everywhere so covered with trees that roots forbade tillage until they had been removed; (4) <u>Minerals</u>, vast beds of iron ore that lay near the surface in loose formation.

Early Uses of the Mesabi

The Mesabi district was the possession of the Chippewa (Ojibway) Indians until January 1, 1855. The native tribes lived chiefly by hunting, using wild game and berries for food. Theirs was a hunting culture. Agriculture as they practiced it was of the most rudimentary sort. Nor did they make use of the white pine or the iron ore that has meant so much to the white man.

Missionaries seeking to Christianize the Indians, and fur traders seeking pelts were the first white visitors. They did not come as did later immigrants, to make homes or settlements, or to conquer the environment.

The Range remained without permanent settlements until the development of mining. A gold rush to the Vermilion Range in 1865 took large numbers of travelers through the district, but these men sought gold--they would probably have had no interest in iron ore even though they had known of its existence.

Lumbering reached its peak on the Mesabi about 1880 to 1890. The lumbermen saw and sought only one resource--pine. The land to them had no other meaning; timber rights were their only concern. Mineral rights were not considered in acquiring the land or in disposing of it after it was stripped of its forests.

Lumbering in the Lake Superior region was carried forward on a large scale. In the early days tremendous loads of logs were hauled in these northern forests. Massive sleds loaded with logs traversed areas in winter over which it was impossible to travel in summer by any type of vehicle. An early observer viewing the forests in what is now the Virginia district thought there was timber enough for hundreds of years, but it was gone in twenty-five or thirty years. An extensive strip of virgin timber near Hibbings believed by early explorers to be inexhaustible, was completely gone in fifteen years after the beginning of the lumbering operations.

Lumbermen left behind only the ruins of their exploitation--stumps, underbrush, and burned-over areas. They did not build a single city of permanence in this forest, not even a permanent dwelling. With the passing of lumber they, like the "lumber jacks," migrated to virgin supplies in the West, or turned to other enterprises in nearby cities. Many timber barons allowed the land to revert to the State to avoid taxes, or sold it for what they could get.

Discovery of Mesabi Ore

Little did the lumbermen know that beneath the roots of the pine stumps they left behind lay buried treasures greater than the entire timber wealth of the nation. Some learned it to their chagrin after having disposed of their landholdings for a pittance; others who held their land because of inability or indisposition to sell it learned of its value to their permanent advantage.

As early as 1850 iron ore had been discovered on the Vermilion Range (some 60 miles north of the Mesabi), by J. G. Norwood. A geological survey in 1864 led to the discovery of the Soudan Mine on the Vermilion Range. As early as 1866 Henry H. Eames, in quest of gold, located iron ore on the Mesabi Range. Peter Mitchell verified his discovery in 1869-1870. Not until 1892 did a railroad reach this range to inaugurate the shipment of ore.

Never before in the history of the world had so rich a bed of ore been located. Moreover, it was found in a loose form, and very near the surface so that mining by stripping with the steam shovel was first employed here. The steam shovel made possible an output without precedent.

This ore apparently had lain undisturbed for centuries. It was potentially a resource of all previous peoples that had inhabited St. Louis County. It was, however, never made an active factor in any previous culture. Why did this resource take on meaning at this time? This question is to be answered only by understanding the impact of a machine age on natural resources.

The Mesabi in an Iron Age

England led the world in iron production in the nineteenth century. Extensive ore discoveries brought America to the place of leadership in the twentieth century. The most important of these was the discovery of the Mesabi deposits.

In 1929 the United States produced 72,199,815 metric tons of iron ore. In the same year France produced 51,028,000 metric tons, Great Britain 13,427,043 metric tons, and Sweden 11,000,000 metric tons. The leadership of the United States not only began with the development of the Mesabi Range but has been maintained by its annual production.

Before 1820 the per capita use of iron in the United States was 40 pounds. This grew to 175 pounds by 1870, and to 400 pounds by 1900. Whitbeck and Finch state in their Commercial Geography that "one corporation in the United States now markets more iron and steel yearly than all the world used in any year prior to 1880. But a century ago iron was a luxury--now it is an 'industrial commonplace.'" In 1907 twelve hundred pounds of ore were used for every person in the United States. Iron has become in a real sense, the measure of civilization in our age. Steel making peoples now dominate the world, and leadership among nations depends upon iron resources.

The iron ranges represent the Industrial Revolution at the raw-materials-end of the process. Activities at the mines represent the first process in steel production. The other end of the process, that of manufacturing the raw material, may be seen at Pittsburgh and other cities. The Range is thus tied up with the commerce and industry of the nation.

The development of the Minnesota Range was a step in the westward trend of the iron industry.

Charcoal was employed in the smelting of iron until about 1850, when anthracite coal came into use. This development led to a great increase in ore production in America, and the industry became centered in the anthracite district of eastern Pennsylvania. By 1875, the use of bituminous coal led to a shift of the ore smelting district to western Pennsylvania and the upper Ohio Valley.

Railroad development during the Civil War period gave the iron industry a great impetus. Soon after (1884), the first ore from the Lake Superior district was shipped. Gradually the ore trade and ore smelting shifted toward the Lake shores. A large steel plant was developed as far west as Duluth and coal for smelting was shipped to the ore, replacing the usual process of shipping the ore to the coal.

The shifting areas of ore production follow the same general trends as do those for ore smelting. In 1899 New York state mined 1,247,000 tons of ore, by 1911 this output was reduced to 1,000,000 due to the competition of Lake Superior area more than to exhaustion of supply. In 1890 Pennsylvania led in the production of ore; by 1911 it held seventh place. The same year Michigan and Minnesota produced more than three-fourths of the ore of the United States. In fact, during that year they produced more ore than the entire United States had produced in 1889. The first shipment from Michigan ranges was 1856, from the Vermilion Range in Minnesota in 1884, and from the Mesabi in 1892. By 1900 the Mesabi Range was shipping over one-fourth of the ore of the Lake Superior district, by 1914 almost one-half, and by 1916 about two-thirds. It has been shipping about two-thirds of the Lake Superior ore even to the present time.

The Mesabi Range came to the attention of the iron men just at the time when inventions for smelting ore with soft coal had reached the place where ore could be profitably mined in the lake district. The time of the discovery was, then, fortuitous. It solved, to a great extent, the problem of raw materials for a rapidly expanding industrial civilization with iron as its basic material culture trait. This industrial need gave meaning to the previously unutilized ore bodies.

Location in Relation to Industry

The resources of the Mesabi have been of first importance to contemporary man. Next in importance, probably, has been location with reference to the heart of American industrial life. We have seen that industrial life gradually shifted westward with the development of techniques for smelting iron by the use of soft coal, until the industry was centered in the bituminous coal regions of the lower lake states. Ore is bulky and the transportation costs are important items in determining the value of a deposit. The location of the Mesabi near the shores of one of the Great Lakes is of the greatest importance.

Ore has been profitably hauled on the Great Lakes from the Mesabi Range to Pittsburgh, a distance of approximately one thousand miles. It is only sixty to eighty miles by rail from the various mines of the Range to lake ports. From these ports ore goes to the lower lake ports by boat and is reloaded on trains and sent to the coal districts for smelting. There is a disadvantage--loading and reloading--but such efficient machinery has been developed that this handicap has been largely overcome. In fact, the ore handling equipment of the Lake Superior district is known as the most efficient in the world.

At Duluth the ore is dumped from ore trains into dock bins, and from the bins into ship holds. At the lower lake ports it is also automatically unloaded and reloaded on the ore trains which carry it to the iron smelting cities. The railroads are exceedingly economical since they are used almost exclusively for ore and can carry the maximum traffic. The loaded trains can coast most of the way from the Mesabi Range to Duluth.

If it were not for these advantages in the way of water transportation and efficient handling, it is doubtful whether the Mesabi ore could be hauled with profit more than half the distance. The Mesabi ore no longer competes successfully with Cuban, Chilian, Newfoundland, Spanish, and Swedish ores in the eastern cities, but so far these cities have not been important competitors.

The Utilization of Other Resources in the Environment

The range cities, recognizing that ore is an exhaustible resource, have tried to plan for the utilization of other resources that will make for an enduring future.

Tourists have in recent years been attracted to the north country during the summer months. While this seasonal trade stimulates business, it cannot assure permanence to the community. The natural resources upon which it depends are also exhaustible. Fish and game, scenery and climate, are the drawing cards. Fish and game conservation measures have to be enforced increasingly to preserve wild life for the future. Cottages and clearings are already marring the landscapes in some sections. Climate will, doubtless, always be an attraction in summer months.

Probably the most permanent type of community can be built around agriculture, for the soil if properly used is inexhaustible. The range towns have recognized the importance of agriculture and have for some twenty years tried to encourage its development. Many Finnish families have turned to agriculture during periods of industrial inactivity or strife, and some have succeeded in making a fair living from the soil, despite the short growing season and the ruggedness of the surface features. One can hardly hope that agriculture will be developed sufficiently to support the towns with their present populations.

Summary

It is clear that the Mesabi, though its resources now appear to be limited largely to ore, has, in the past, provided for other types of adjustment. For the Indian it was a hunting ground; for the lumberman it was a country to exploit and abandon; for the present generation it is a land of permanent settlements where man can live by mining ore; for the Finn it is a land where agriculture is possible; for the tourist it is a paradise of lakes, fish, scenery, and climate--a place where he can find recreation and rest.

The adjustments made by each group have depended upon its cultural possessions. The various natural resources of the Mesabi have taken on meaning to resident groups only as their culture patterns have been able to utilize them.

Chapter III

POPULATION IN RELATION TO CULTURAL ADJUSTMENT

It was a select group of people that answered the call to mine ore on the Mesabi. There has been an element of selection in all subsequent migrations, but uniqueness in population has tended to disappear as the cultural adjustment has become more complete. The population has gradually approached the American norm in its composition and characteristics.

The Population Perspective

The Range represents an association of conglomerate peoples such as is found only in the most cosmopolitan centers in America. They have gathered to the Mesabi from forty or more nations over a period of forty years. Wave after wave of immigrants has come soon to be absorbed into the Range civilization. The daring, the adventuresome, the lonesome lumberjack, the seasonal immigrant who at first returned annually to his homeland in Europe with his savings, the gambler, the outcast who wanted to hide from society, the prostitute, as well as the respectable and the elite--all these have come.[1]

On the other hand, there were men born "to hustle," men who were foresighted, men who were first in exploiting the earth's treasures; capitalists and engineers, and the middle class of merchants and professional men. Of such characters have been the migrants to this community which offered work for the untrained, the unamericanized, and the uncultured, as well as for the energetic, enterprising, and venturesome. They were men who came to exploit, not to cultivate or to conserve.

Phenomenal Growth of Range Towns

The Range towns were boom towns. Their rapid growth is without precedent in Minnesota history. In eighteen years Virginia reached the 10,000 population mark, and in twenty-eight years Hibbing passed the 15,000 population mark. In 1900 Eveleth bade fare to become the largest town of the Range, as it then exceeded Hibbing in population; however, it gradually fell to third place in size. Eveleth reached her numerical climax in 1910, and Virginia in 1920. Hibbing grew slightly during the last census period (1920-1930), but the rapid growth of previous decades has not been duplicated. Virginia lost over 2000 of her population during the last census period.

Disproportionate Number of Males

The sex ratio of a community is important not only from the biological standpoint, as it relates to the maintenance of a normal population increase, but also from the psychological and sociological viewpoints as it affects the mental stability of the people and determines the trend of cultural development.

The Range towns originally drew the male sex, many of them young venturesome men without worldly possessions. The hazards, uncertainties, and risks of this pioneer front did not attract women in any great numbers, and even the men attracted were heavily sprinkled with the Bohemian type who either had few family attachments, or who were willing to sever family ties in the hope of bettering their position or of acquiring new experiences. Women came later, when the communities bade fair to be suitable places for home and children.

Even after the towns had been in existence two years, the ratio of males to females was five to one. The original census forms for the 1895 State Census list fifty-three Virginia women as "demimonde," and three as "prostitutes." Thirteen Hibbing women were listed as "sports." Many men were also of questionable character, nineteen being listed as gamblers in this first census of Virginia.[2]

The lack of civic pride, the prominence of vice in the field of leisure-time activities, and the laxity in governmental control, all of which characterized the Range towns during the first ten years of their existence, can be better understood when interpreted in the light of the sex ratio then existent.

Birth and Death Rates Gradually Approach Normal

Immigration has been an important factor in the population of the Range towns, not only because of the numbers added, but also because of the high reproductive rate of the immigrants. For some twenty-five years the birth rate on the Range was excessive as compared to that of other communities. Gradually with the passing of the years, the immigrant groups have reached the second generation and birth rates have declined until they are comparable to other American Communities.

In the early years death rates, especially among infants, were very high, but they declined rapidly after 1910. The high proportion of young people in the communities; until very recent years, has made for a low death rate.

Excess of Violent Deaths

The number of violent deaths has been high on the Range. This is to be expected in a community predominately masculine, where men face the hazards of industry. The accident rate in mining is taken up in another chapter, so it is sufficient to state that previous to 1910 the accident rate was especially high. A report from the Virginia Enterprise of April 29, 1904 is suggestive. It reads:

> There have been 160 accidental deaths
> on the Range during the past year. Of this

number, thirty-five lost their lives in mine disasters, twenty-two died of alcoholism and nine met death by gun-shot wounds. The remainder represents suicides, victims of skull fractures, men who were crushed in the woods and those who died of exposure to the cold or were drowned or cremated.

Statistics prepared by Alexander Hamilton, deputy clerk of the district court, prove interesting in that they give a fair idea of the number of risks run daily in the work on the railroad. In the vicinity of Virginia there were eight deaths in railroad accidents and eleven in the mines, one from gun-shot wounds, one from opium poisoning, one sawmill accident, two deaths from alcoholism, six suicides, one murder and one death from exposure to the cold.

At Eveleth, alcoholism claimed two, a fractured skull caused the death of one and a broken neck another.

There were a large number of deaths at Hibbing. The railroad caused thirteen, the greatest number of fatalities. Mines stood next with twelve, two of which were from suffocation. Whiskey came next with eleven victims.

Suicides

The suicide rate in the Range towns has at times been excessive as compared to that of the United States registration area. This was, generally speaking, truer previous to 1910 than later, although since that time these towns have had fairly high rates.

The uneven distribution of the sexes in the early days very likely had a bearing upon the high suicide rate.

A newspaper account of a 1903 suicide case is typical of a good many of the early reports of suicides. After the statement of the subject's death the account reads:

> Christianson came here from Hibbing about a year ago, and for several months was employed as porter by Ed Finch. He was discharged on account of dissipation, and since that time has been employed at various places.
>
> He was intoxicated at a late hour Tuesday night, Deputy Coroner Lenest says that death had occurred about twelve hours before the body was found which would time the commission of the deed at about six o'clock Wednesday morning. It is supposed that he was despondent over his habits and consequent inability to secure work.
>
> So far as known he had no relatives in this part of the country. The body was removed to Hesberg's morgue, from which place the funeral was held. [3]

The suicide rate among single people previous to 1910 was much higher than that for the married people, but since that time the suicide rate for the latter group has increased.

The recent high rate among married men suggests that economic difficulties have been a factor, although the suicides are not grouped in the months when the mines are most inactive, but are quite evenly distributed throughout the year. It is possible, however, that economic factors have had a bearing, and that a good proportion of the cases have been among the chronically unemployed.

Immigrant Population

The population of the Range towns is an amalgama

tion of many nationalities. The Northern Europeans, the
English, Cornish, Welsh, Austrians, Irish, Finns, Swedes,
and Norwegians came first. Then came the Italians and
other Southern Europeans.

> The babel of more than thirty different
> alien tongues mingles with the roar of mine
> blasts and the crash and clank of machinery.
> Here side by side work Finns, Swedes,
> Montenegrins, South Italians, English, Irish,
> Bohemians, Frenchmen, Hollanders, Syrians,
> Belgians, Croatians, Danes, Russians,
> Magyars, Bulgarians, Germans, Greeks,
> Scotchmen, Welshmen, Dalmatians,
> Norwegians and Servians· [4]

The population of Hibbing in 1910 was 50 percent
native born; the balance was foreign born. Practically the
same ratio obtained in Virginia. By 1920 the ratio was
about 65 percent native to 35 percent foreign born. Hibbing
had 77 percent native born population in 1930, and 23 percent foreign born; Virginia, 73.2 percent and 26.6 percent
respectively, Eveleth had 70 percent and 30 percent respectively.

Data on the total foreign population of Virginia, with
the percentage for each nation, for the three census years
1910, 1920, and 1930, are available in the United States
Census. The dominance of the Finnish and Swedish elements for each period is noteworthy. The Norwegians also
rank high. Though the Austrians ranked high in 1910, they
have constituted a small percentage of the population since
that time. "Virginia is more of an American town than are
the other towns," is a comment frequently heard on the
Range, or "Virginia is a 'white' town." Southern European
immigrants are not considered white folk by many of the
local residents.

Comparable data are available for Hibbing for 1920
and 1930. The Finnish element constituted over a fourth of

the immigrant population for both census years; the Swedish element constituted about 11 percent. Southern Europeans rank high. The two leading southern European groups were the Italians and the Yugoslavians, which together constituted approximately 32 percent of the foreign born population in 1920 and 35 percent of the foreign born population in 1930.

Although statistics are not available for Eveleth,[5] it is generally conceded that her population is more predominately South European than that of either of the other Range towns.

Conclusion

It is clear that though the Range population has in the past been abnormal in most of the characteristics by which populations can be compared-- numerical increase, age groups, sex ratio, marital status, birth and death rates, violent deaths, and nationality composition--by 1940, if recent trends persist, the population will approximate the American norm in most all respects.

As the culture of the Range has approximated the culture of other American communities it seems that the population also has approached the American norm. Advancing material culture was doubtless a factor in attracting new residents to the Range, who in turn effected important social and cultural changes.

Footnotes for chapter III

1. See Part III for a description of some of these types.

2. The original census schedules are on file in the Documents Department of the State Historical Society at St. Paul.

3. The <u>Daily Virginian</u>, January 23, 1903.

4. Hodges, L., "Immigrant Life in the Ore Region of Northern Minnesota," <u>Survey</u>, XXVIII, p. 703.

5. Under 10,000 population and therefore not analyzed in the reports of the United States Bureau of the Census.

PART II

GROUP ADJUSTMENTS DURING THE HISTORY OF THE RANGE

Chapter IV

THE PIONEER PERIOD

"The country was newly settled by vigorous, adventurous men." Life centered in a struggle against nature. There was no time for the petty conflicts of civilizations characterized by leisure. Class stratification had not developed. The two dominant groups, capitalists and laborers, worked together to conquer the rugged hills, to span the swampy flats, to sink mines, to build railroads, and to establish homes and cities.

The characteristic spirit of the three infant Range towns is suggested in the box head which appeared on the front page of each issue of the Iron Village Sentinel during the year 1894-- "Man was born to Hustle." The frontier presents no other alternative unless it be to perish.

Hibbing was founded in 1893 by Hibbing and Trimble. Their portable sawmill converted the virgin pine into lumber for dwellings. Soon homes were erected, residents came, a railroad was built,[1] and business men opened headquarters.[2] During the first season more than a hundred test-pits were sunk within a radius of three miles of the town site, and the existence of an abundance of ore was assured.

A description of the infant village, Eveleth, and its surroundings as they existed in 1893 is paraphrased from an article in the Iron Age:[3] There were not more than 15 buildings in the place all told and there was not one stock of goods, wet or dry. Various new mine pits, a hotel, the paint of which hadn't yet dried, and a bank whose fixtures hadn't arrived, made up the town. With such a beginning Eveleth, then only ten months of age, had shipped between 500,000 and 600,000 tons of the most excellent ore.

Virginia at the time of its founding, presented a picture of pioneer energy and tenacity. The town was only well started when a forest fire broke out in the vicinity. Soon it had reached the edge of the settlement of wooden buildings and in "forty minutes after the first shack caught fire" the entire village lay in ashes. Many left the town; the suicide rate rose rapidly, but the majority remained to rebuild the town. Reconstruction was begun immediately. A description of the one public building which housed the services for the religious, recreational, social, and sensuous needs of the community during the winter after the fire suggests the character of life. In it were held all "indoor gatherings, church services, minstrel shows, dog fights, socials, bacchanalian carousals, and gambling events." On the ground floor next to the sidewalk was the village barber shop. The central room was a saloon, in the rear were gambling dens and in the back was the Enterprise office. On the upper floor public meetings were held. At one end was a platform on trestles of beer kegs. [4]

Economic difficulties soon added to the troubles of the frontier villages. The panic made itself felt in 1894. It was difficult therefore for promoters to borrow the necessary money for the large investments which had to be made in railroads, clearing, test-pitting, and opening of mines. Moreover, the large bodies of ore discovered were said to have actually frightened investors. They feared that the supply of ore was now so great that the market would be flooded and the product would become practically worthless.

The work for which laborers had come to the Range was not to be found. Idle men walked the streets of the towns for want of employment. Hibbing sent out this notice through the Sentinel in April of 1894.

"The laborer who hasn't anything else to
do might just as well keep away from Hibbing.

> We have enough unemployed--good and husky
> men who are ready and more than willing to
> work-but the fact is that there are two appli-
> cants for every job, where only one is hired. A
> man with a little money can by judicious
> investments soon double it in Hibbing. A man
> without money is likely to play in hard luck."

In Eveleth, men who had formerly been employed in
lumbering and test pitting at $40.00 per month and their
board could not get a day's work. The iron business was at
its worst.

The Mahoning mine paid $40.00 to $60.00 a month
to its few employees at this time.

> After pay day a Mahoning miner was
> looked up to with respectful awe in Hibbing,
> and the less fortunate ones speculated on
> whether he could buy a railroad, a line of
> steamships or go to Europe for an extended
> vacation. [5]

Fires threatened each of the towns repeatedly
during the summer of 1894. The grasshoppers ate up the
gardens and crops. Many residents left for the Dakota
wheatfields or other more favorable localities. A Range
editor after having lived in the midst of these experiences
commented in September:

> In the presence of forest fires and other
> calamities without end, it is somewhat difficult
> to work up the proper enthusiasm over politics.
> This has been a wonderful, fateful, and disas-
> trous year. Every day we hear of some new hor-
> ror in the way of railway wrecks, mine disas-
> ters, of holocaust, and we begin to think with
> Professor Totten and others who believe in the
> Visible signs that the end of the weary old
> world is not far off.[6]

The darkness of this period, however, soon disappeared. Midwinter lumber camps had taken up all surplus labor to harvest the timber deadened by the forest fires. The "lumber jacks" were paid only $6.00 to $12.00 per month, but at least they were given work. But by the middle of 1895 the depression was forgotten and each of the towns was being built rapidly, and the spirit of optimism was in evidence everywhere.

Buildings were being erected in Hibbing at the rate of three new structures a week. The hotels were crowded nightly with newcomers. Population increased at the rate of 100 per week. While sinking the city well, ore was struck, indicating that the entire city was underlaid with a rich bed of ore.

Virginia also boomed. "We have seen," said the editor of the Enterprise, "Virginia grow from an insignificant crossroad neighborhood to a population of five thousand in as many months; we have seen it left as a barren and desolate waste of fire's destructiveness and have seen it rebuilt and again become the only town on the range, as the result of the united and determined efforts of its enterprising citizens. We shall also see it become the first city, the only city and the distributing point for nearly or quite all the business of the entire range." [7]

Eveleth did not share fully in the prosperity of the nineties. People did not believe there was much ore in the vicinity. "I had some disappointments," comments its founder, "with my early townsite enterprise. The influence of so many nonbelievers in the existence of ore in the southern part of township 56, section 17 had its effect-- when I plotted your now beautiful city Eveleth." [8]

The fact was, Eveleth had been plotted over the best ore deposit in the district. Important developments did not take place until 1900 when the town was moved one-fourth of a mile uphill to permit the opening of the Fayal mine.

It appeared, by 1900, that pioneer difficulties were over, but this did not prove to be the case for Virginia. On June 7 of that year a fire broke out in one of the new mills and destroyed nearly all of the business section. Many people left, but others stayed to rebuild the city.

"The rapidity with which Virginia is rebuilding," said the editor of the Enterprise, "after its second disaster is a matter of much surprise to visitors to the city. With the new walks laid and the buildings completed and occupied which are now in course of construction, the new Virginia will present the handsomest most substantial town of the Ranges thirty days hence." [9]

This prophecy was literally true. On the first anniversary of their fire he was able to write.

> Where but one year ago were the smouldering ruins of the second Virginia, today stands the only brick city of northern Minnesota. Practically all the burned buildings having been replaced with handsome brick structures, filled with finer stores and happier homes, as a result of the well-placed confidence in our future. [10]

The newspapers previous to 1900 depict struggling mining villages on the Mesabi with life full of irregularities. Numerous accounts of suicides, fights and drunken brawls, deaths from exposure of homeless men in drunken stupors, accidents among laborers in the mines and woods, reports of criminals being captured who had fled from other cities to the Range mining centers to lose their identity among pioneers, cases of the passing of counterfeit money, printing and forging mining and lumber company checks, jumping rooming-house board bills and hotel bills, the operating of "blind pigs" to avoid paying the liquor license--all these appear as news items.

Hibbing was so accustomed to the sensational, that

in a week of 1899 when things had been rather "dead" the press reported, "There are no deaths, births, marriages, mining accidents, suicides, runaways, fires, elopements, stabbing affrays, or scandal reports this week."

During this early period there was no serious conflict between the industrial group and labor or the public. The mining industry was considered the foundation of life in the area and company rights were seldom challenged. The people having come to a mining settlement, they expected nothing better. Even when the strike of 1894 was brought about by agitators who had come into the Range from other mining centers, little local cooperation was obtained from the miners. Moreover, the business men in the towns threatened to withhold credit from the strikers if they continued to oppose the mining companies. These friendly relations toward the mining companies were maintained until about 1910.

The Transition from Pioneer Society

Soon after 1900 the three towns were assured a permanent existence. The following decade was characterized by a gradual transition from pioneer to permanent society. The nonmining public increased in the population. This group, being a normal one composed of married men with wives and children, demanded conveniences and respectability of the community in which it lived. This group fought against the vulgar elements in community life, and eventually succeeded in bringing about the eradications of pioneer vices and in increasing local conveniences.

During this transition Virginia presents the most intense struggle for reform in morals.[11] As early as 1895, a Finnish Temperance Union was organized. Steps were taken by the city to close houses of prostitution, gambling dens, and to remove slot machines. By 1902 dice and cards were specifically banned. Of course, it was impossible to enforce the laws entirely, but their enactment gave evidence that the moral development of the town was a matter of concern with a small public.

Moral reform got into politics around 1906. The struggle of parties sponsoring or condemning vice characterized every political battle for the following eight years. Some elections were won by the vice crusaders; others by candidates favoring a "wide open" policy.

Hibbing, like Virginia wrestled with the problem of pioneer vice. Prostitution had been pretty well obliterated there by 1906 through the enactment of a statute which banned brothels from the village. Gambling, however, was a recurrent evil.

The town boasted of sixty-five saloons in 1909. The editor of the Ore suggested that these should be cut to about twenty-five and made to pay a license fee of $1500 to $2000.

Here an element not found in the other-towns, was injected into the saloon situation. For a long period there was considerable discussion as to whether Hibbing was in the territory in which saloons were prohibited by an early Federal treaty with the Indians. From time to time between the years 1905 and 1915 saloons were closed and reopened by special acts of the State and Federal courts. After one such closing of a few days duration, it was reported that twelve carloads of beer were shipped in to relieve "the dry spell." [12]

After the Indian treaty had failed to banish liquor from the town in 1911 a vote was taken on the matter, which resulted in 1,160 votes for licensed liquor, and 295 votes against it. The total village receipts for the year amounted to $327,238.80 of which $32,150 was from liquor licenses. This may have been a factor in swinging the vote.

Moral reforms came late in Eveleth. A civic league

was organized in 1905 with a membership of 700. Its purpose was to secure law-enforcement-- especially anti-saloon and health regulations. The number of saloons was limited to one for every five hundred people, and all were to be closed at eleven every evening and all day on Sunday. Crusades against slot machines and the location of the red-light district were initiated by the league with the result that slot machines were banished. The red-light district was finally segregated and later driven out of the city, but not until several years after it had been outlawed in Hibbing and Virginia.

All in all, respectability was costly in the mining towns. With the development of standards of respectability came the accumulation of desires for comforts and luxuries. These same groups that demanded respectable morals, turned next to exploit the mining companies through taxation to gain recognition in material culture. They sought privileges and luxuries for themselves, their children, and for the worker.

In 1908 the newly-elected president of the Virginia Commercial Club, a recent comer to the Range, called attention to the fact that the city then had between nine and ten thousand residents, yet had no public parks, no playgrounds, few trees, few lawns, and no flower gardens. He urged cooperation to the end that the citizens might see their city develop through an increase in public improvements.

Soon Hibbing also was to adopt a new municipal policy. The conservative president of the village, Dr. Ray, was to be replaced by a man of the people, Victor Seabold, who was to transform the village which had been suggestively described as a "cross between a rat hole and a mud hole" into what was claimed to be the most wealthy, most lavish, and most famous village in the world.

Eveleth likewise, even sooner than the other towns, shook off the crude municipal properties of her youth and set the pace for the Range in public works and luxuries.

The development of the desire for conveniences, services, and respectability proved to be cumulative in nature,
and soon led the communities into conflict with the industrial tax paying group.

These new desires on the part of the public were des-
tined to disrupt the friendly relations existing between mining company and community; reform groups and political
classes within the public became integrated against the
common foe, absentee capitalists. Thus, the conflict interaction pattern came to characterize the second period in the
history of the mining towns.

This period in Range history is covered in the next
chapter.

Footnotes for Chapter IV

1. The Duluth, Mesabi and Northern railway reached
   Hibbing, Oct. 25, 1893.
2. A compilation of business enterprises at the close of the
   first year showed the following: five saloons, five hotels,
   three grocery stores, two meat markets, three real-
   estate dealers, two contractors, one lumber yard, one
   hardware store, a dry goods store, bank, and a jewelry
   store.
3. See LVI, p. 593.
4. See Van Brunt, Walter, History of Duluth and St. Louis
   County, p. 589.
5. The Sentinel. April
6. Ibid., Sept. 1.
7. Feb. 8, 1895, p. 4.
8. Van Brunt, Walter, op. cit., ch. 22.
9. The Virginia Enterprise, Sept. 14, 1900.
10. Ibid., June 7, 1901.
11. The history of the political struggle presented here is
    based on news items taken from the bound files of the
    Virginia Enterprise.
12. The Sentinel.

Chapter V

THE PERIOD OF CONFLICT

The second period in these mining communities was characterized principally by a struggle between the mining companies and the local public for possession of a share of the economic benefits attainable from the mining of iron ore. Labor took a position with the public so need not be considered separately. The industrial group consisted of the corporations developing the natural resources. The public was composed of the residents of the cities who found expression and unity of action in governmental organization. In the struggle between these groups, the corporations sought profits. Political groups, representing the public, desired taxes to be converted into public works and services by which the community might be enriched.

A summary account of the struggle between the industrial group and the public is presented in this chapter. It seemed best to confine the picture largely to Hibbing. This permits a more detailed description than would be practicable should the struggle in the three towns be thoroughly reviewed. Moreover, Hibbing represents the conflict pattern most clearly, for there the conflict has been overt and may, therefore, be observed readily.

Suffice it to say, however, the conflict pattern has been present in Eveleth in a very overt form and especially so during the last fifteen years. In Virginia the conflict has been much more subtle. In fact, Virginia has not represented, in some respects, the typical mining-town culture, probably due to the fact that she has depended on other industries than mining, notably lumbering.

Hibbing Defies the Mining Companies[1]

The conflict between the mining companies and the public gathered momentum years before it broke into an open struggle. The integration established during the hazardous periods of the founding of the communities disappeared very slowly.

The people in Hibbing elected Dr. H. R. Ray to the village presidency for six successive terms previous to the overt expression of the conflict. Dr. Ray cooperated with the mining companies and carried out a conservative program as far as public developments were concerned. Because of his connection with the hospital, where mining companies carried contracts for health service for their men, Dr. Ray was naturally interested in maintaining friendly relationships with the mining companies. The townspeople were led to feel that they owed their existence to the mining companies, and must, therefore, keep their good will.

During the last year of President Ray's administration, however, sentiment against him began to accumulate, preparing the way for a new administration.[2] Victor L. Seabold, an attorney and prominent citizen, seems to have been the leader in condemning the mayor and council for their backwardness in city development.

Mr. Seabold later ran for the presidency and carried the election of 1913. His election ushered in a new regime for Iron Village. He was reelected nine consecutive one-year terms. During this long administration he was never seriously challenged in an election.

A program for elaborate municipal expenditures was planned under Mr. Seabold's leadership, and for ten years the city spent money in a highhanded manner, defying the mining companies and the law. Seabold proved capable of meeting every attack of the mining interests and won almost every city-mining company legal encounter during his long administration. Under Seabold's leadership the village gained a national reputation for public works.

Backing their new mayor, the commercial club decided in 1913 that the best way to get trade by the newly completed interurban line and to bring people to Hibbing was to make the village the most beautiful one on the Range. The following day the City Council planned for a great deal of additional paving and lighting.

However, the Lake Superior Tax Association was formed during the same year by thirty-one mining companies. Its aim was to secure more reasonable expenditures for municipal improvements. The association affirmed a friendly attitude toward the villages, but was interested in getting improvements economically.

Overt conflict between the village and the mining companies originated in damage suits brought about because the mining companies blasted too near the residential districts of the town. Seabold had been the lawyer in these original suits, and attained enough recognition as a result of victories to carry the village election.

The newspaper historians claim that the blasting had greatly retarded development of the town. The streets could not be properly lighted for fear that the blasts would destroy the lamps. The streets and sidewalks were not paved because the mining companies might some day take over the entire village and convert it into a mine pit.

The village had heretofore remained in subjection to the mining companies, as many citizens felt that the companies were their greatest benefactors because they provided for their very existence. They also held that if an attack were made upon the mine operators they would stop operations in the district and concentrate their efforts in other districts, thus leaving the people without employment. Victor L. Seabold took the opposite position. He announced that the people were less dependent on the mining companies than the companies were upon the people, and further said that in case the mines were shut down in the Hibbing district, he would simply assess the maximum tax upon the company properties, and start enough public works in the village to keep all idle men employed. Later, when the occasion came, the mayor enforced this threat to the letter. The mining companies stopped operations in the immediate vicinity for a season, and during this period there were almost as many men on the village pay roll as there were voters.[3]

In retaliation the mining companies refused to pay their taxes for the latter half of the year 1913. Seabold made various attempts to secure legislation that would compel them to pay; he also tried to get the Governor to seize their ore stockpiles. The companies fought back by getting injunctions passed which hindered municipal building projects temporarily. They were not, however, successful in checking expenditures for any great length of time.

In November, 1913, the News reported that Hibbing lived up to its reputation of a million dollar village by employing expert advice at a cost of $12,250. This advice uncovered laws that led to the redemption of $13,000 from the township, due Hibbing for certain annexations. During the same year the city spent $41,181.09 on parks, boulevards, and other city improvements.

The mining companies made a bold stroke in the Harrison Bill which was introduced into the legislature to limit municipal expenditures to 50 per capita. A delegation from Hibbing and from the other towns attended the hearing at St. Paul, and by a heroic effort Seabold succeeded in getting the measure defeated. He returned to Hibbing, where he was banqueted and treated as a hero. He was known thereafter as the Napoleon of Hibbing.

The conflict between the village and mining companies again came to the surface in 1917, when the mining companies instituted an injunction restraining the village from paying certain bills.

Following this injunction, the mayor and councilmen were tried for graft, having been charged with the presentation of fraudulent claims. The first two officials tried were declared not guilty, so the other indictments were dropped without trial. The Hibbing press commented upon the trial as an attempt on the part of the Steel Company to "railroad" Hibbing officials to prison. Seabold was given credit for the victory over the Steel Company.

Another angle of the conflict came to focus in the moving of Hibbing.

The actual moving of the village came, for the most part, during the years 1918 to 1920, after the remodeling of streets, lighting, and public buildings had been completed. The moving was described in the local press as the most gigantic operation of its kind that had ever taken place anywhere.

The occasion, cost, and method of moving the city is well described in the Historical Edition of the Hibbing Daily News and Mesaba Ore of October, 1921. The mines had so encroached upon three sides of the town that the business district was left on a peninsula surrounded by mines. The problem was to obtain a new place for the people to live and for the business establishments to operate. The Iron Mining Company purchased eighty acres south of the original town, and moved their employees' homes to the new site. They allowed the merchants to choose their sites in New Hibbing. The company then built three modern business blocks and sold them to the merchants, helping them to finance the purchase. The cost of the project of moving is estimated at $16,000,000.

In old Hibbing, the Seabold administration had built a city with pavements, white ways, sidewalks, water and sewer systems, and public buildings. These utilities were scarcely completed when they were destroyed. The mining companies wanted the ore under the city and, of course, were expected to pay again (they had already paid most of the cost of the improvements through taxation) for all village property that was to be destroyed. There is considerable evidence that Seabold did not go into the matter blindly. He, and all other residents of Hibbing, knew that in the not distant future the town was to be moved. Apparently this was a matter for mining companies to worry about.

But the victory was not entirely one-sided. The moving enterprise had far-reaching implications for Hibbing. The mining companies purchased only a part of the town area. Two-thirds of the old townsite was not purchased, so stands today on the brink of the world's largest iron mine. Property values have been greatly deflated. Business has been ruined for the only approach to the city leads through the new and better Hibbing, a mile south. The village has, since the move, been divided both in spirit and in physical autonomy. Seabold lives in the memory of many as the man who "sold out" his village.

Hibbing Submits to the Mining Companies

When one studies the trend of events since 1925, it becomes increasingly evident that the position of the combatants is being reversed. The mining companies are becoming the dictators of the policies which the village must pursue. The mining companies' victory was won in the reduction of village expenditures through legislative restriction. The per capita limitation law became effective in 1921, and was modified to further reduce expenditures in 1929.[4]

Village administrations have since found it well nigh impossible to keep expenditures within the limits of the per capita law, but when they have attempted to exceed these limits they have been threatened with injunctions by the Lake Superior Tax Association, a mining-company organization.

When townsmen in Hibbing saw that they were

defeated by the mining companies, they floated a
$2,000,000 bond issue to cover a part of the indebtedness.
The total indebtedness of the village in 1921 was approximately $6,000,000.

The conflict with the mining companies, carried on
by Mayor Moss for the village since the moving of Hibbing,
has centered in an attempt to obtain damages for property
holders and business men in the Southern and Pillsbury
additions in old Hibbing. Attempts have been made
annually under one claim or another by organized groups of
citizens to receive damages for lost property values from the
mining companies through judicial decision or through
legislation, but all in vain. The matter was even carried to
the United States Supreme Court in 1927. This struggle
makes an interesting story as it has been reconstructed
from newspaper files, but one which is too long to recapitu-
late here. The significant point is that Hibbing has lost the
fight. It is learning to bow, even though unwillingly, to the
mining companies.

Eveleth Buys a Reputation
Through Athletic Achievements

The overt conflict due to extravagance in Eveleth
took a rather peculiar turn. It came later than in Hibbing,
reaching its climax in 1923. Eveleth set out to achieve
athletic supremacy at city expense. The pattern was not
new on the Mesabi. It had been customary for the towns
from early days to buy baseball talent in order that they
might be able to show up well in the league games.
Beginning around 1912, the athletic program was broad-
ened in all the Range municipalities. The towns took on
extensive recreational programs sponsoring winter sports,
carnivals, hockey, and curling. These programs reached
their climax in the building of elaborate recreational buildings in memory of the World War heroes.

Perhaps the outstanding stroke in attracting athletic

talent to Eveleth was the hiring of Bob Taylor, World's champion curler, who since his coming has won twelve state championships for the city.

A man by the name of Pratt introduced curling on the Range. For some reason the game took hold of public interest rapidly. Soon all of the Range towns had teams and had constructed large indoor playing spaces. Eveleth built the recreational building primarily for the curling club, and put Bob Taylor in charge of the building as a city employee. By this means she supported the world's champion curler and developed a whole generation of curlers, for Taylor not only has cared for the building but has also taught the game.

Another big stroke in athletic advancement was effected through the bringing together of a professional hockey team. Most of the men comprising this team were imported from Canada, and were supported in the city for their prowess in the game. This team gained a reputation for the town. It played in the national championship finale losing only to Cleveland, Ohio. Of even more significance was the fact that in 1928, Eveleth was asked to furnish a hockey team to represent the United States at the Olympic Games at Amsterdam, Holland.

The material side of the hockey complex found expression in the building of a giant hippodrome, which was alleged to have been the largest indoor rink in the world. After this building was abandoned the sport was carried on in the recreation building.

The building of athletic space and the support of players, as well as the expense of the games, required large amounts of municipal funds. It was the problem of recreational expenditures that lead to litigation and overt conflict.

Harry Purim, a local resident, brought charges against the city officials for having spent money illegally in building the hippodrome. Purim was a mining-company sympathizer, his father having once owned a mine. Local informants suggested to the writer that Purim was also incited by mining companies. At any rate, he pushed the suit against the city officials and in 1923 secured their conviction.

Some $64,000 in obligations to a lumber company for materials used in the building of the large hockey rink, to a hotel for the care of visiting athletics and their wives, and for other general promotion expenses were charged to the account of the city officers on the ground that they had illegally expended this amount of public funds for sports.

Other questionable actions of city officials, discovered by Garfield Brown, State Public Examiner, resulted in 1923 in the removal from office of Mayor Camack and councilman Van Kuzkirk by Governor Preus. Eveleth and the Range revolted against this action by the Governor, maintaining that since the city was under a home-rule charter, the Governor could not remove officers without legal proceedings. The city officials remained in office, and the following November they were reelected by a big majority. The community accepted them as "martyrs to the cause of the local community," for they were leaders in the fight against the millionaire capitalists of the East.

This was only the beginning of difficulties. Repeated accusations of graft have been brought against various councilmen and Mayor Camack. These officers have been indicted by grand juries, but only one councilman has been convicted. He was sent to prison. The same administration that has been accused of the most graft was still in office in 1935.

Repeated injunctions against the cities spending more than the per capita limit have been instituted by the mining companies. As a result the city has operated by issuing warrants against the following year's budget. In 1930 the city failed to pay the proportion of back debt required by the per capita law, so the mining companies were instrumental in imposing an injunction limiting expenditures to $30,000 per month until a stated percentage of the outstanding indebtedness was paid. City affairs are still being conducted in a highhanded manner, but Eveleth too is bowing to the mining companies.

Virginia Capitalized Prosperity

Virginia has not been accused of extravagance as the other Range towns have. She has built extensively and expensively, but has gotten dollar for dollar value for her citizens from her public works. Even the mining companies have not objected strenuously to expenditures of this nature. During the period when Eveleth was squandering money in municipal recreation, and Hibbing by the paternalistic policy of employing needless labor and the careless use of funds in public office, Virginia was developing her municipal ownership program adding a municipal gas plant, the first on the Range, and extending city heat to practically the entire city.

Money was laid aside for public building projects, with the result that in 1924 a beautiful recreational building and city hall were completed on a strictly cash basis. Virginia built conservatively and has never spent more than $40.00 per capita,[6] so is unaffected by the per capita limitation law.

In Virginia the conflict has been primarily between political groups and not between the public and industry, though there is a subtle conflict, which has never appeared on the surface, existing this relation.

Footnotes for chapter V

1. This story of the Hibbing mining company conflict is
   constructed from news items taken from the bound files
   of the Hibbing <u>Daily Tribune</u>. For a brief summary of the
   conflict for the years 1912 to 1920 see the historical
   edition of this same paper published Dec. 31, 1921.
   See also Howard, A. S., <u>Hibbing, The Old and The New</u>.
   1920.

2. See the <u>Hibbing Tribune</u>, Mar. 30, 1915.

3. See ch. X.

4. See ch. XI.

5. This account is based largely on news items found in the
   bound volumes of the Eveleth <u>News</u>.

6. Estimate made by City Clerk, Ford, of Virginia in an
   interview.

Chapter VI

THE PERIOD OF STRUGGLE FOR SURVIVAL

This third period in the history of these mining towns will undoubtedly be characterized by abandonment and cultural decay. Industrialists will remove their enterprises and laborers will leave the scene when the basic resource can no longer be mined profitably. The nonmining public will be left behind. Members of this group will have vested interests in the continuation of the society. Their homes, fortunes, and emotional attachments will be tied up in the local community. An intra-group struggle will probably ensue and ultimately determine those who can survive in the old setting.

This final period will be similar to the first period in one respect. Society will be characterized by a struggle with nature for maintenance. However, it will not be labor and industry struggling together to make a resource available as in the first case, but it will be an intra-group conflict within the public. Again, it will not be a struggle to develop an abundant resource already known to exist as in the first case, but it will be an effort to develop resources that are in themselves neither attractive nor inviting.

The Mesabi has not entirely reached this stage as yet, so most of the generalizations regarding this period are more in the realm of prediction than in that of history.

In speculating on the final phase of the life cycle of mining-town culture, two lines of evidence are followed. The first is found in the adjustment measures employed by the towns in times of industrial depression when labor could not be depended upon for business and trade. At such times two types of adjustment have been attempted--the development of an agricultural hinterland and the attraction of a tourist trade. In each adjustment the public has taken the initiative. As the exhaustion of the ore approaches undoubtedly attempts to develop these two activities will be intensified by the town merchants.

A second line of evidence is found in the adjustments which towns that have been partially abandoned have made. The only important example on the Mesabi is Gilbert, which is discussed later. It presents significant adjustments that are suggestive of the final period in the history of the mining town.

Just when the Mesabi will reach the final period one cannot accurately foretell, but it is a certainty that its days are numbered.

Let us turn our attention now to a study of attempts at adjustment that give some hint regarding the possible future activities of the Range town public.

Building a Trade Hinterland

The Range municipalities have made concerted efforts to develop agriculture in the surrounding hinterland for some twenty years or more, realizing that in times of industrial depression, and in case of the future depletion of iron ore, their hope for survival lay in more permanent industries.

Economic conditions of the winter of 1912 stimulated an intense interest in agricultural developments among business men of the Range. An address given before the Hibbing Commercial Club at that time suggests the prevailing conditions and developing sentiment for agriculture. It reads in part:

> I do not believe that Hibbing will ever again see the prosperous times that made us the most talked of town in Minnesota several years ago. Then there were drills working all

over the iron fields in this section employing
skilled labor at high wages and unskilled labor
at much better figures than was the run elsewhere. Stripping operations were everywhere
busy and exploration work of all kinds was
going on. Contrast that condition with the one
of today. There remains to be done little exploration work in this vicinity. Where there were a
hundred drills working here a few years ago
there are not a half dozen now. The open pit
mines here are nothing more or less than huge
stock piles. There is enough ore bared to keep
the steam shovels busy for years, and the stripping operations in this section are not to be so
large an item hereafter as in the past. New
ranges are developed and the mining industry
in the future, so far as it affects Hibbing, will
be governed largely by the steel market.
Sometimes it will be busy and again it will be
dull. This has never since its inception been a
city of homes in the strictest sense of the term,
but it is becoming more so. The man who is
interested in Hibbing in a business way and
who intends to live here does not have to go far
into this matter to find that what we need is
more farmers...[1]

This sentiment has grown yearly with recurrent
industrial depressions and unemployment. Farmer's fairs
held annually in each town, the St. Louis County Fair, held
at Hibbing, booster campaigns, advertising campaigns,
carried out under the supervision of the commercial clubs,
potato warehouses for the storage of crops, creameries,
special potato trains exhibiting Range products, and other
devices have been used to stimulate interest. The mechants
rather than the farmers have backed all propaganda for
agricultural developments.

Each town has tried to cater to rural interests and
rural trade. For instance, Eveleth carried the slogan on a

recently issued Commercial Club folder, "Eveleth--where agriculture and mining meet." The Eveleth News published a special farmer's day historical edition, September, 1922, describing farming in the hinterland and extolling the developmental possibilities of farming and dairying. The Virginia Queen City Sun carried the following box heads during the summer of 1932. "A wild acre of land is a liability to the State and to this community. A cleared acre of land is an asset. Encourage the farmer to clear his land."

Virginia merchants seem to have a particular awareness of the importance of capitalizing their trade possibilities. This is suggested in the comments of the merchants as one discusses the future with them.

The comments of the business men are more optimistic with regard to agricultural developments than past trends justify. There has been very little increase in rural population for years in St. Louis County. The strike of 1907, in which the Finnish anarchist group took the leading part, drove thousands of Finnish miners to the soil. During this strike the mining companies imported Southern Europeans as strike breakers, and for several years after the strike they discriminated against Finns in selecting employees. The increase in rural population from 20,531 in 1900 to 47,211 in 1910 is explained to a considerable extent by this situation. Since 1910 there has been comparatively little increase in rural population in the county. Between 1910 and 1920 there was an increase of 7.8 percent, but between 1920 and 1930 there was a decrease of 4.9 percent.

The rigorous climactic conditions of St. Louis County, the rocky soil, and the almost unconquerable underbrush make one wonder if any peoples other than sturdy European peasants, who have never known anything but hardships and poverty, would possess the patience necessary to wrest a living from most areas in the County.

Baiting a Tourist Trade

A second enterprise which the Range towns have encouraged, chiefly through commercial club propaganda, is the advertising of the hinterland as a summer vacation center of unusual attractions.

The three Range towns are in the heart of the great "Arrowhead District," the so-called "Playground of the Nation." Virginia and Eveleth are on roads leading to the various Lakes and resorts: Eveleth is the first city the tourist strikes on his trip north from Duluth, the "Tourists' Gateway to the Mines and Lakes Country." Hibbing is on the highway that leads into the arrowhead district from the southwest. More than 5,000 tourists pass through the Mesabi Iron Range towns annually.

The Range towns raised $30,000 in the fall of 1926 with which to advertise the Arrowhead District. Each of the towns has circulated attractive folders since 1930, baiting tourists with pictures of lakes, fish, golf courses, scenery, iron mines, magnificent public buildings, and swimming beaches.

There is good reason to believe that as mining declines at some future time, tourist patronage will be sought increasingly.

The Leach Town

Gilbert is located in the center of important ore reserves, but reserves on which the mining companies hold long time leases. Years ago, after the mining location had grown to a prosperous city of some 3,500 population, the mining companies left the field to work deposits on which they held short time leases. This meant the complete abandonment of mining activities for several years; labor left the city. Ore bodies are taxable even when they are not being mined, so iron ore taxes were still available to the public.

When the mines closed, many of those business men who kept their places open turned to vice for maintenance, and an abnormally large number of the rest of the public turned to city and school employment made possible by ore tax revenues.

During the days of national prohibition the combined saloons and brothels flourished on the proceeds they received from the patronage of the neighboring mining towns. The town was easily accessible from all Range points, and "parties" there were likely to be safe from interference by authorities, although there were four or five fully uniformed policemen on the main street every night. In fact, one could walk a block or two and pass only policemen. It is certain that they made no attempt to curb illicit activities. Occasionally Federal men visited the community, but these visits were usually communicated beforehand to the resort owners by the usual "grapevine" method, with the result that the Federal men succeeded in padlocking only one or two places at a time. A visitor going through main street in 1933 could observe four places of business with padlock notices on their doors which had been closed because of the violation of the Eighteenth Amendment.

If the resorts of Gilbert had depended on local patronage, they would have been closed long ago. The local residents know what goes on behind the curtained windows of the "soft drink" parlors, but they have built their homes in good faith and naturally are reluctant to dispose of them when values have shrunk to almost one-fifth of the original figures. Most of the sporting-house owners are of Southern European stock. Today the patrons are the younger men of the Range communities, out for a "thrill," and traveling business men and other "respectable" men from distant points seeking secluded revelry.

The situation in Gilbert represents a readjustment that takes place where labor is gone, but where taxable resources are still present, so it is not exactly typical of

the final period in the history of the mining town. It is,
however, suggestive of the fact that new adjustments are
made when labor, one of the three basic groups, leaves.
If ore had been previously exhausted, a large part of the
public that now lives by tax incomes would have had to
either seek a new means of livelihood or migrate. As conditions now exist, only the business men have had to make
new adjustments. The successful arrangement was found
in carrying on two forms of illegitimate business, boot-
legging and prostitution, both of which drew trade from a
large hinterland.

How Long Will Ore Last?

In the exploitation of Mesabi ore the policy has been
to take the best first. Disregarding this fact for the moment,
it is significant that Eveleth had in 1930 passed the mid-
way point in ore supply, Hibbing had approximately
reached it, and Virginia had exhausted only a small portion
of the supply within the city limit.[2] The figures for Virginia
are deceiving, however, as the most active mine of recent
years is just outside the city limits in the territory of the village of Franklin. The building of Virginia had been partially
due to this mine, from which a large portion of the best ore
has been removed.

It took thirty-eight years to reach this stage of
development. How long will it take to exhaust the supply
in Eveleth, Hibbing, and Virginia, excluding the possibility
of developing ore bodies that are not now merchantable?
Basing estimates upon an average of the annual productions of iron ore for the five years, 1926 to 1931 inclusive,
we find that if ore is produced in Hibbing for the next
seventeen years and four months at the same annual rate
at which it was produced for the above period, the known
supply of merchantable ore of 1930 will be exhausted.[3] On
the same basis, ore in Eveleth will be exhausted in approximately twenty-two years and in Virginia in one hundred
fifty-five years. According to the average annual rate of

shipment that has persisted for the five years, (1926-1931) the present known bodies of merchantable ore of the Mesabi will be exhausted in thirty-two years.

The prediction for Virginia is high. This is due to the fact that mines did not operate in Virginia during the five years used as the base period, with the exception of the Minnewas Mine, which began operations in 1930 and shipped over a million and a half tons during the season. [4] At the 1930 rate of production, Virginia ore supply will be exhausted in fifty years.

There have been years when the Mesabi has produced less ore, and years when it has produced more ore, but the average annual production for the fifteen-year period, 1916-1930, has been 35,031,332 tons. At this rate, the supply of ore will last only thirty-three years. The average annual production for the thirty-year period, 1901-1930, has been 28,612,456 tons, which means that if this same rate persists, the ore will last only forty years. Even if we take the average rate of production since the first ton of ore was shipped from the Mesabi and assume that future productions will average no more, Mesabi ore will last only fifty-two years.

The most conservative prediction, based on the past developments, indicates that by 1980 the Mesabi will be stripped of all its present known supply of merchantable ore. In fact, an estimate based on production of the last fifteen years, which probably indicates more nearly future conditions, suggests that the good ore will be exhausted by 1963.

The quality of iron ore on the Mesabi Range has decreased from 56.07 percent iron in 1902 to 51.19 percent in 1929. For the last ten years, however, the quality has remained about constant, due largely to the use of various "beneficiation" devices.

Estimates place Minnesota's possible lowgrade ore

reserves at 40,300,000,000 tons, or approximately one-half of the known world supply of ores that are at present considered non-merchantable in their Natural state. [5] The low-grade ores that will be used first are those that can be mined by the cheap open pit method. Most of these ores are on the Mesabi Range. It is estimated that there are 9,447,500,000 tons of low-grade ores on the Mesabi that can be mined by open pit methods and "beneficiated." [6] These ores average about thirty-five percent iron and are found to a depth of 400 feet, but most of them cannot be "beneficiated" by known methods. However, inventions may not be far distant which will make this possible. There is also the ever-present threat that tax rates will make "benefication" unprofitable, and that new and more distant fields can be exploited with greater profit.

Wherever one places his estimate, regardless of the degree of success in developing low-grade ores, it is obvious that the days of the Mesabi towns are numbered. The greatest iron range of all history will some day, perhaps during the next generation, be worthless and desolate. Its technological culture will doubtless fade away gradually.

Footnotes for chapter VI

1. Hibbing News. March 1, 1912.

2. See Minnesota Mining Directory, 1931.

3. Ibid.

4. The Mesabi Mountain Mine in the village of Franklin, borders the city limits of Virginia, and has been the largest ore producer in the world. It has produced an average of approximately five million tons annually, 1926-1930, and has a remaining tonnage of over twenty-three million.

5. Warner, F. S., Future Movement of Iron Ore and Coal in Relation to the St. Lawrence Waterway, 1930.

6. Lake, M. C., Mining and Metallurgy, Aug., 1926.

PART III

CULTURAL CHANGE IN THE MESABI TOWNS

A. Pioneer Folkways and Mores
B. Culture Building During the
   Period of Extravagance

Chapter VII

A. Pioneer Folkways and Mores

THE REALISTIC NATURE OF PIONEER FOLKWAYS[1]

The first concern of men who are facing nature in the rough is to supply basic organic needs. The primary necessities, food, shelter, and sex satisfaction are first provided. Extras, in the way of material improvements, come later.

Food

Fortunately for the pioneers the North woods was bounteous in game, fish, and wild berries. Both lumber and mining camps always had deer and moose meat, regardless of seasons or laws. Eveleth residents were said to have lived mostly on moose meat during their first winter.[2] Fish were secured by all known means--nets, dynamite, and by less wasteful methods. Later, communication was established with the outside world so that food from many areas could be shipped in. The ability to purchase food shifted attention to earning and spending wages.

Industry

The prospectors preceded the settlers and located ore bodies. The extent of the deposits were for the most part unknown. The method of test pitting was crude compared to later methods, but required an extensive output of human energy. A well was sunk in the stony soil by means of pick and shovel, and the refuse was windlassed out. The forests had to be shaved from the surface of the soil, shafts sunk for bringing out the ore, and railroads extended to lake shore points some sixty miles away before ore could be marketed at the lower lake ports a thousand miles distant. Individual enterprisers with large capital reserves backed these projects so that labor was provided with work and wages.

Merchandising

The mining company store provided necessities in pioneer days. Newcomers to the Range needed credit, as well as food, clothing, and tools, and the companies could furnish it in return for labor. The company store was in the nature of a monopoly, and quite often charged exorbitant prices for foods and mining supplies. Companies frequently required the men to buy at their store even after private merchandising had become the rule. The month's expense account was deducted from the pay check.[3]

Because there were wages, merchandising became profitable, and a merchant class appeared in the mining towns. As early as 1898, merchants in Hibbing protected themselves against the company store, and against the companies which designated certain private stores as the places for their men to trade. An unsuccessful move was set on foot for securing legislation to make the company store illegal. The company stores, however, rapidly disappeared after 1900.

Range prices were reputed to be high. A protest was registered in the Sentinel of October 12, in 1895 to the effect that citizens were paying twenty cents for kerosene while most places in the state were paying ten cents and fifty cents for potatoes while Princeton, Minnesota, paid ten cents. Editorial comment suggested that the difference could not all be attributed to freight rates. A commercial public had apparently arrived to exploit labor.

Shelter

Shelter was a serious problem in northern Minnesota where frosts are likely to occur monthly and where winter temperatures frequently range far below the zero point. Even in summer, nights are cool and rainfall is heavy. Nature provided fuel in abundance, thus solving this problem for the settler.

The men who plotted the Range towns brought with them fixtures for small sawmills; so construction began with the clearing of the town plats. Some of the buildings were made of logs, but most of them were made of unplaned lumber which the mills provided from virgin pine forests. A common type of dwelling was the boarding house where a large number of male residents lived.

The towns were characterized by board sidewalks, ungraded streets, and crudely constructed outdoor privies. Even the business blocks were of frame construction--poor guarantee against the forest fires that ravaged the woods during dry seasons, or even against fires that might originate within the towns.

Sex Satisfaction

In the nineties the Range population was largely men who had left their families in the old country or in their former homes in this country. The primitive life attracted a large number of the unmarried from abroad as well as from more settled parts of America. These men came to the Range lured by the opportunities a mining community offers: hard work, attractive wages, and the hope of stumbling onto a fortune.

The pioneer communities were, in their inception, communities without homes. Few women with families ventured there. Those married men who had families did not bring them until the basic needs of life were provided. The frontier, however, proved to be a favorite spot for women who commercialized sex.

The prostitute substituted for home and family for married men of the pioneer mining communities. She furnished satisfaction for all male groups.

Relaxation

In the same wagons that carried the prospective miners and lumbermen to the North country and in the same crowds traveling on foot were the liquor merchants with their wares of trade, the gamblers carrying their games and devices, and the prostitutes. Almost every other building that was erected on the main streets of the towns housed a saloon with its backroom gambling dens and upstairs quarters for the prostitutes. There seems to be a correlation between primitive mining communities where hard manual labor is the means of lucrative employment and equally intense and vicious forms of amusement. The Range fits this picture.

It used to be the custom of the single men in the boarding houses to hurry off to the saloons Saturday evening and arrive home just in time to change clothes and report for work at the mines Monday morning. The chief amusement center provided was the saloon.

As the basic needs of life were met, men turned toward conveniences, developed civic pride and community consciousness. This desire gathered momentum as the non-mining public increased in the Range communities. Soon new material culture sprang up to break the hard realities of the frontier.

However, as long as the pioneer characteristics of the communities remained, the fundamental problems of their residents of a few years later were of no concern. City halls, public works, pavement and utilities, recreational facilities, parks, playgrounds, and ornamental culture, libraries and brick school buildings, tax rates and tax levies, were little thought of by the pioneers. In fact, the State did not consider an adequate tax on iron ore until 1907.

Footnotes for chapter VII

1. See Ch. 5 for a summary of historical data on which most of the generalizations of this chapter are based. Also Woodbridge, op. cit.; Van Brunt, op. cit.

2. Van Brunt, op. cit., ch. 2.

3. This was one of the issues of the strike of 1907. See ch. 13.

Chapter VIII

THE TOLERANT NATURE OF PIONEER MORES

Many men who were attracted to the Mesabi frontier had probably never been dominated fully by the mores of any community. This is indicated by the frequent reports of escaped convicts, thieves, men who had deserted families, and those who for other reasons had sought the seclusion of the mining camps. Notwithstanding there were undoubtedly others in the lot who had previously maintained high personal standards and had demanded reputable mores in the communities from which they had come. But standards suffered in the mining camps, and many forms of behavior were tolerated, if not directly sanctioned, that would have been condemned and outlawed elsewhere. The coming of complete families in considerable numbers alone changed the frontier codes.

Let us consider briefly behavior traits that reflect pioneer mores.

Respectability of Saloon Keeper and Saloon

The saloon owner of this day was considered a respectable business man of the city and was a very powerful figure in the administration of its affairs. He controlled politics in the city of Virginia through the "lumber jack" vote in the early days and was to be reckoned with in every election. Early settlers tell of the streets being crowded with drunken "lumber jacks" in the spring of every year, who had received their winter's earnings and boarded the first train to the town to get to the saloons as soon as possible. The women were there to receive them and encourage them in drinking at the bar. The "jack" would wake up three or four days later with a splitting headache and empty pocketbook, having been "rolled" by the bartenders or female hangers-on around the saloons. Then the penniless "Jack" would be kicked out of the saloons because he no longer possessed resources for exploitation by their agents. The streets and saloon fronts would be lined with penniless "jacks," with nowhere to go except to the city jail, there to be lodged and fed at city expense. On election day they were treated to drinks and told how to vote.

One reason for the respectability of the saloon is that there was no other community center to which homeless men could go when the day's work was done and on holidays and Sundays. Consequently men gathered there not only to drink but to spend their social evenings. While hard drinks were sold, many a man patronized the bar only to buy soft drinks. To be seen swinging the portals of the saloon was not considered below the dignity of the respectable citizen. The drink itself doubtless had its attraction for the majority of the patrons. The Sentinel reported in 1895 that over a carload of "Fitcher's Beer" was consumed daily in Hibbing. There were thirty saloons in the village at that time, and they were reported to be increasing at the rate of one a day.

It is interesting to note that with the coming of the moving picture theater, saloons declined considerably in popularity in the Range towns.

Accepted Behavior

A news item from the Sentinel of February 22, 1894, indicates that drunkenness was accepted as the commonplace.

There is a false idea afloat in foreign towns that the residents of mining districts are no respectors of law and order and are generally tough. We are prepared to nail that false belief by an illustration from Hibbing. Thursday, February 15, was pay day at several of the mines and also at the mill. It is needless to say that the boys all "took in the town" and enjoyed themselves to the full limit, and yet not a single arrest was made, nor a complaint registered. The boys were out for a time and had it, and we can say, from personal knowledge, that they were more gentlemanly drunk or sober than a party of swell "guys" of the city would be under the same circumstances.

A similar comment from the press of March 15, 1894, indicates that the election of that time must have been pretty well celebrated. It reads:

With 200 inebriated men election evening, it is strange there were no accidents. Everyone seemed to "feel their oats" but no arrests were made and nothing occurred worthy of note.

The standard of morality was none too high. According to the news story the entire village flocked down to the station once a day to see the train come in. "Passengers, male and female, were subjected to a gauntlet of remarks, some of them not free from profanity and innuendo, as they alighted from the train." [1]

Prostitutes in those days, according to informants, did not seclude themselves from public view in daylight on the streets. There was no shame in their vocation, for a considerable part of the female population could be labeled demimonde.

Prostitutes were not respected by all but were, apparently, tolerated. An editorial in the Hibbing Sentinel of 1894 (June 2) suggests that the editor was not fully in accord with the toleration policy. He comments:

The charge against Mrs. Hannan of
keeping a house of prostitution was dismissed
in Justice Robinson's court Tuesday--and
mighty rank "justice" everybody thought it to
be.

Tolerance of Illegal Enterprises

Games of chance were always in violation of the law,
so gambling dens were, from the beginning, subject to raids
by county officials. Many an expensive roulette wheel, slot
machine, or other gambling device was seized in the towns.

The Grand Jury, meeting in Duluth in 1899,
reported:

We find that the president and council
of the village of Hibbing have allowed and
suffered gambling to be carried on openly in
several saloons and hotels of the said village;
that gambling devices of the most common and
notorious kind have been allowed to be openly
exhibited in said saloons and hotels and that
they have been used for the purpose of gambling and that they have been maintained for
the purpose of getting the laboring men of the
village and locality to waste and squander
their earnings; that the village has been infest-
ed with professional gamblers and confidence
men from the whole Northwest and in the
opinion of this jury the village has become the
rendezvous of the crime and corruption of St.
Louis County; that this state of affairs has
been made possible by reason of the consent,
sufferance, if not the assistance of, T. Walde
Murphy, the president of the village, and A. A.
French, policeman and night watchman.[2]

Later, $2000 worth of gambling paraphernalia was

taken in a sheriff's raid on five places, and fines totaling $604.65 were inflicted.

In addition, there were the illegal boxing matches, forbidden by state laws, and enforced by county officials. Nevertheless, the mining towns had their boxing matches frequently.

Even the sale of liquor in Hibbing was for a time forbidden by law due to an early Federal treaty with the Indians, but it was only when Federal enforcement officers were on the scene that saloons were closed.

Low Evaluation of Life

Protection of life reaches its highest development where there is feeling of responsibility for others. A male community treats life carelessly and blots it out more freely. The Range communities had suicides altogether out of proportion in the early days, many unnecessary industrial accidents, and deaths from intoxication and exposure. The following glimpses from news items suggest the nature of the situation.

Brown had dinner at Daigle's hotel, after which he declined to go out to camp and complained that he was sick. He was supplied with a bed and Doctor Butchart was summoned and prescribed for him. On Monday the man died and was removed to Barrett's Morgue by order of Deputy Coroner Walker, who examined the body and decided that an inquest was unnecessary. The deceased was about forty years old and nothing is known of his friends or relatives. There was nothing of value on his person and the only inkling as to his name was the employment agent's card which was made out to Geo. Brown. The body will be buried today.[3]

A man about forty-five years of age fell down a shaft and was instantly killed.

The deceased had worked at the Pillsbury only a month or so, and there is no information as to the where abouts of his relatlves. [4]

An old logger is quoted as saying:

But the old days when we came down from the woods were glorious ones. For the first week we always owned the town. The constable and sheriff either had business about that time in some neighboring town or locked themselves up in their houses. The wild dissipation we indulged in and the amount of villainous whiskey we consumed would kill anyone except one possessed with a constitution such as a winter's campaign in the woods insures. The boisterous laughter and the maddening yell must have been anything but reassuring to the peaceful citizens. To their credit be it said, however, those rough loggers were as a rule a good-natured gang, and did not molest anyone unless some overzealous officer attempted to interfere. Then there was trouble. The way a good part of the winter's wages was squandered in a few days was a shame....After a spree we often went back to work on the drives. Of all the work I ever did, log driving was the hardest....Submerged wholly or partly in ice-cold water with no chance to change clothes, there is little wonder that we all have rheumatism until we are certain our backs are broken and that our arms and legs will drop off. A busy summer at the mill a visit to the harvest fields and in the fall we were back again in the woods. Lucky if we had a good knit suit and sufficient clothes. [5]

Protection

Industry was careless with men in the early days on the Range.[6] Primitive justice in settling personal quarrels was frequently resorted to. There were few provisions for caring for health and few regulations to protect a man against the vices into which he had fallen. Life from the protective standpoint was very much on an individualistic basis on the frontier; therefore, casualties were numerous.

Religion

The mining frontier had little interest in religion; work was the dominant interest. It is true, however, that missionaries soon came to the mining camps and attempted to give them the sanctity of religious worship. Little data exists regarding the nature of religious work on the Mesabi in the nineties, but suffice it to say that the press of the time gave it little prominence.

Democracy

All men had status in these frontier communities. There was no noticeable discrimination because of caste or class. Race and nationality, religious creed, moral code, and fraternal attachments were awarded no prizes and brought no disgrace. Anyone who could work was an accepted member of the community, for numbers meant more than quality.

A Finnish lady, a long-time resident of the Range, in an interview gave the following analysis of the change in nationality sentiment:

Regarding racial prejudices, there was little difference in races or nationalities in the pioneer days. All were interested in making a living and in building up the community. Hard work was the order of the day, and a man was accepted for face value according to his contribution to the community, not his religion or nationality. As leisure time has been diffused among the laboring classes the nationality prejudices have manifested themselves. Today each nationality is highly conscious of its superiority over the others. Each nationality has its societies, and every year sees these activities and societies grow stronger and more popular.

Shaking Off Pioneer Mores

As life became more stable, the old mores here gradually condemned and were slowly replaced by new codes.[7] The morals of the mining towns had been loose. The second decade saw prostitution and gambling banished, the Sunday and all-night saloon forbidden, the number of saloons limited to a given unit of population, and pure food laws introduced.

Life took on new meaning to the residents--the careless exploitation of labor, the careless licentious living, and the low evaluation of life gradually disappeared. The masses gradually became aware of community independence from the mining industry. They came to demand a share in ore aside from wages--the benefits that come through protection, taxation, and public services. In this manner they prepared the way for the lavish culture built during the conflict period.

Footnotes for chapter VIII

1. Miles, Carlton, "The Romance of the Ranges," Minneapolis <u>Journal</u>, May 2, 1926.

2. Hibbing <u>Sentinel</u>, November 11.

3 The <u>Sentinel</u>, 1899.

4. <u>Ibid</u>.

5. <u>Ibid</u>., Jan. 29.

6. The accident rate was excessive on the Mesabi until around 1910

7. See the latter part of ch. 4

Chapter IX

B. Culture Building during the
PERIOD OF EXTRAVAGANCE

COMMUNITY GRATIFICATION THROUGH PUBLIC SERVICES

In contrast to the primitive folkways of the pioneer period, the conflict period in the Range towns saw the growth of extensive public works and the building of lavish public institutions. These developments are significant indices of the folkways of the period. In this chapter a brief survey of the material culture of Range towns is made with a view to indicating the extent to which public services were developed for the citizens of the municipalities. The most important municipal services are: public utilities, educational facilities including schools and libraries, and recreational facilities. These are discussed in the order named.

Public Utilities

Since around 1912 no one of the three Range towns has lacked anything in the way of ordinary public utilities. In addition to cement sidewalks, which replaced the board walks of pioneer times, the streets were paved and after that was accomplished the alleys were paved. Not only were streets lighted with electricity, but elaborate white ways with five lights to the lamp post were laid out to decorate the cities. At the close of the Seabold presidency Hibbing boasted of more white ways than could Cleveland, Ohio, a city over twenty-five times as large. Not only were mechanical fire trucks purchased, but fire halls were built, and enough firemen were employed to have three shifts, each group working eight hours. (Most other cities at that time were working two shifts daily, each group working ten hours.) Hibbing and Virginia each built municipal gas

plants where artificial gas was produced. Beautiful city
halls were erected. Greenhouses were built to provide flow-
ers and shrubs for the parks. Zoological parks were established in each municipality and stocked with animals.
Public rest rooms were provided for the farmers. Municipal
nurseries were established for the children of working
mothers. Hibbing went so far as to build potato warehouses,
where the farmers temporarily disposed of their potatoes.
The village in turn took the responsibility of sending them
to the local merchants. Besides these warehouses the
city maintained a municipal barn and a market place.[1] On
July 4-5, 1931, Hibbing dedicated a 160-acre municipal airport. Virginia also has an airport, valued at $87,000.

Perhaps the outstanding achievement in public
works has been the development of municipal heating
plants in each of the towns. In Hibbing and Eveleth heat
has been largely confined to the business sections; Virginia
has extended heat to residences in all parts of the city
except the section north of the railway tracks.[2]

It is also Virginia that has achieved national
recognition for the successful operation of municipally-
owned public utilities. It had the lowest electric rates in
America in 1931.

Education

Educational institutions have grown both in
numbers and in architectural grandeur in each of the
Range towns. During pioneer times school buildings were
small frame structures that soon became overcrowded
because of the high birth rate among immigrant families.
As the years passed and the large numbers entering the
primary grades gradually rose from grade to grade, buildings had to be erected almost annually. It was estimated
that in 1932 the peak load for the high school would end
and that thereafter the number of high school pupils would
decline.

The population factor is back of the material development of the school system. There are other factors such as the growth of community pride in public buildings, financial prosperity, extravagance mores, inter-range-town rivalry, etc., that help to explain the type of school buildings that were developed.

The population aspect of the school program suggests that in the near future there are likely to be vacant school buildings, fewer teachers and a complete cessation of the building program, thus reversing the growth trend that characterized the school systems of the three Range towns until 1930.

The school building program was at one time hindered somewhat by mining company protests. However, the tonnage tax agitation in 1909 did considerable to get the mining company's support for better schools. The Range people joined hands with them to fight the tonnage tax, the proceeds of which were to go to the State treasury. The argument used was that such excessive State taxation would rob the Range schools of their necessary support. At this time the mining companies sanctioned the building of a high school; also of two frame structures for primary schools.

The Hibbing Junior college came in 1921-1922 and grew rapidly from an initial enrollment of forty in 1921 to an enrollment of 350 in 1931. Teacherages have been built in the outlying locations of the district. Busses have been employed to bring students to the centralized schools. Texts, paper, pencils, and musical instruments are provided by the schools. No tuition is charged, even in the junior college.

The Hibbing School District (Number 27) covers six full townships and eight sections of a seventh township. It is twenty-four miles long and twenty miles wide. The assessed valuation is $28,000,000, about 95 percent of which is derived from the iron mines located in the immediate vicinity of Hibbing. Hibbing claims to have the largest and most costly high-school building in the world. This building has a frontage of 416 feet and has three wings, the longest of which is 265 feet. It has two gymnasiums, a swimming pool, large study hall, library, splendid auditorium, botanical conservatory, large cafeteria, the general offices of the school districts, a suite of rooms for the school dentist, doctor and nurses, and open-air rooms for pupils of frail health. There is a ten acre site for athletic grounds in the vicinity.

The curriculum includes the following: foundry, forging, machine shop, automobile and gas engine, agriculture, assaying, mineralogy, surveying, printing, normal school training, biology, physics, chemistry, botany, bookkeeping, typewriting, shorthand, art, music, sewing, cooking, millinery, dressmaking, mathematics, history, engineering, geography, Latin, French, Spanish, economics, and civics.

A phase of education not found in the ordinary community, but one which is highly developed in the Range towns, is adult education and citizenship training. Probably in no other section of Minnesota has adult education been carried to such perfection as in these towns. This is due to the large number of Europeans who have been drawn to the mines. Those responsible for education soon realized the necessity of Americanizing these foreigners. Every school district can boast of an enviable record in their Americanization programs. No expense on the part of the schools was spared; every possible facility was utilized. Civics, American government, United States history, and English were the principal subjects taught.

Second to the school system only are libraries in the scheme of Range education. Each of the towns has libraries housed in well-built brick buildings, that provide books in many languages, a special children's reading room, and special parlors for club meetings and social gatherings. In each town the library developed after the passing of the pioneer period, and reached its peak during the period of extravagance in culture building.

The traveling library plan, which has attracted nation-wide interest to the Hibbing library, is unique. The traveling library bus or "Book Wagon" is six and one-half feet wide, fifteen feet long and six feet high. It is built to carry twelve hundred books and seats ten people, including driver and librarian. Benches are placed in it back to back for the use of customers, drivers and librarian. In its travels the bus covers an area of 160 miles reaching twenty-five locations. Most of the locations are visited once a week; a few of the smaller ones are visited every other week.

Municipal Recreation Facilities

Beginning about 1912 the Range cities took on an extensive recreation program sponsoring winter sports, hockey, curling, and winter sport festivals.

Each town, previous to the per capita limitation law, financed baseball, and hockey teams. Eveleth built a combined auditorium, armory, and community recreation building in 1912 at a cost of $25,000. In 1918 a recreation building for skating and curling was erected at a cost of $125,000. In addition a hippodrome of wooden construction built on huge dimensions was erected. The other two towns followed with combination recreation and auditorium buildings in memory of the World War dead.

Dances seem to be the order of the day insofar as recreation is concerned. The recreation building in Virginia has four or five dances every week--ten cents admission and four hours of dancing. Eveleth has the same. Hibbing has very little dancing in the summer, but frequently has ten-cent municipal dances in the winter.

The dance floors of the recreation buildings in the three towns are converted into ice-skating rinks during the winter months, although they have hardwood floors; they are covered with roofing paper and sand and then flooded. The Hibbing arena has a composition floor which is flooded during the winter months. Adjoining the rinks are heated rest rooms. In addition to the arena there are outside skating rinks in practically all the school yards throughout the cities.

Due to the large financial resources of the Range school districts, all schools have built the most modern and fully equipped gymnasiums, swimming pools, athletic fields, and auditoriums. Great stress is placed upon school athletics. No expense is spared to get the best coaches and instructors. Swimming instruction is given the year around in the two pools in the Virginia schools.

Then, each town has well-developed parks. The Eveleth Memorial Park, containing six acres, was laid out in 1913. Here the library is located and here weekly band concerts are held in summer. Another park, located on the north side, is primarily a children's summer playground. The tourist park is located on Eveleth Park Lake, overlooking St. Mary's and Eveleth Lakes. Here swimming facilities and equipment for camping are provided. The facilities of the tourist camp are available to all at a daily charge of fifty cents. In 1911 the Oliver Iron Mining Company donated fifty-five acres to the city of Virginia to be used as a park. This area became Olcott Park, and the city immediately planted it with trees and shrubbery. Some 10,000 trees were planted, thirty-five miles of boulevard laid out, flower gardens prepared, and a zoo arranged, turning the area into a playground and recreation center. The South Side Park was opened a few years later. Municipal band concerts are held twice a week during the summer months in these two parks.

As early as 1905 Virginia had established a public park system. In the reorganization of the government in 1909 a Park Commission was created to have charge of the park system.

Early in 1915 visitors pronounced Hibbing park system the best in the state, considering the expenditures involved. Conrad Wolf, an expert landscape gardener who was park superintendent under the Seabold administration, is given much of the credit for its development. The Mesabi Park was located in the heart of the village and the Bennet park, south of the village. Since Hibbing was moved, Bennet park stands between North and South Hibbing. Here is a public greenhouse, a zoo, flower gardens, shrubbery and trees. It is an ideal recreation center in good weather, wood and fireplaces being provided for picnics.

The greatest private venture in Hibbing recreation was the Oliver Club, established by the Oliver Iron Mining Company in 1908 and opened December 25. This provided a recreation center for Oliver employees of the district. A similar club was established in Virginia about the same time.

The Hibbing recreation budget voted for 1926 amounted to $34,479.91. A salary of $3,500 was paid a sports director, and $2,500 each was paid a man and woman assistant.

Summarizing, the culture of the period of extravagance presents a contrast to that of the pioneer period. Public utilities, which were of little concern to the pioneers, were extensively developed during this time.

Footnotes for chapter IX

1. See also historical editions of newspapers in each of the towns.

2. See <u>Minnesota Municipalities</u>. 1931, pp.226-229; 280-285; 292-294, for number of customers and rates charged for various utilities in the three towns.

Chapter X

PERVERSIONS IN SPENDING

Communities whose social classes do not contribute equal shares to tax moneys find it difficult to get the most in returns from public expenditures. This is especially true when conflict is the dominant attitude existing between the spending group and the tax-paying group. We wish now to consider perversions in spending that seem to grow out of the conflict relations between the industrial taxpayer and the spending community.

It was in the year 1912 when Victor Seabold came to the presidency of Hibbing as the choice of the people that extravagance began. Previous to this time the office was held by Dr. Ray, a conservative man, who was associated with the hospital which received the workingman's monthly health fees through the Oliver Mining Company. The attitude had prevailed in the village that the Oliver Company was the best friend the community had, and that the people should strive to maintain friendly relations with it. Citizens had put up with inconveniences and dangers to maintain the harmonious relationship, but Seabold, in taking an antagonistic attitude, brought the conflict to the surface.

In three years Seabold had multiplied expenditures more than four times. Hibbing had become more than a million-dollar village. An official of one of the mining companies commenting upon Seabold's administration in an interview with the writer said, "They could have paved the streets out of silver dollars here for all the money they have grafted."

Note the change in expenditures under the old and new regimes.[1]

COMPARATIVE EXPENDITURES

Year	Expenditures	Receipts
1910	$ 303,152.13	$ 333,850.02
1911	282,292.25	340,751.86
1912	484,960.10	327,979.09
1913	773,062.10	417,125.07
1914	1,233,728.54	902,789.76

A mining-company politician called attention [2] to the fact that for a ten-year period Hibbing, a village of 15,000 population, spent more than Duluth, a city of 100,000 population. He said further, "Many illegal expenditures are permitted in the Range towns that would never be permitted in any other towns."

A large indebtedness began in Hibbing with Seabold's presidency. Continued additions brought the total to approximately four million at the close of his ten-year term. Obligations totaling $3,428,344.00 remained in January, 1931. [3]

Eveleth also had a period of extravagant spending which led to the accumulation of burdensome debts. Obligations totaling $463,959.00, [4] were revealed by an audit in January, 1931. The public examiner, on reviewing the books in 1929 [5] found that the city was about one year behind in paying current bills. It was making no provision for the payment of outstanding debts, although the expenditures in 1930 could not exceed $70 per capita. The city had also suffered a loss of $4,000,000 in valuation in the preceding ten years.

The mining companies, in a report to the State Tax Commission in 1928, presented the following statistics on obligations of mining towns in Minnesota.[6]

PER CAPITA MUNICIPAL INDEBTEDNESS

Municipal Indebtedness:	1925	1926	1927
Mining District	234.51	220.89	200.41
Balance of Minnesota	65.33	-	-
Entire United States	75.06	-	-

It is apparent that municipal expenditures have been lavish, even to the extent of exceeding the abundant tax revenues.

The extensive development of the material side of education came about after 1910. This development coincides with the appearance of the dominant conflict pattern. To secure greater benefits from ore, for the public and for labor, lavish expenditures carried developments far beyond the point of necessity. The common question with school boards came to be, "How much can we spend?," not "Where can we save?" As one Range superintendent expressed it, "In other communities where I have worked the basic question at all board meetings was 'Where can we cut expenses?' Here the first question is, 'Is that all we can levy?'" [7]

As a result, the fame of Range education has spread far and wide. People who know nothing more of the Mesabi towns have heard of their schools. The traveler in even the smallest range municipality is amazed to see its beautiful and costly school buildings. Virginia claims to have one of the finest technical high schools in existence; Eveleth has a similar one, and Hibbing has achieved school fame by owning what is alleged to be one of the finest high school structures in the world.

Expenditures have not stopped at the legitimate and legal. Public works for which there was no legal authority in municipal charters have been constructed and managed.[8]

There is considerable evidence that Hibbing and Eveleth politicians have tried to extend public services gratis to many. Eveleth had eight paid engagements for the auditorium and 350 gratis engagements for 1916, while the recreation building records showed one paid engagement and 110 gratis engagements.[9]

The Eveleth water department, in 1929, had fifty-one customers on its free list, had large sums in uncollected bills, and was operating at an annual net loss of $32,583.33.[10] The same situation obtained in Hibbing for many years.[11] In many cases a discount of 50 percent was allowed on bills.

Range towns have acted like individuals who suddenly fall heir to immense wealth, and spend lavishly, even seeking new fields of expenditure to dispose of their money. Each town is the center of immense ore reserves, which in themselves create a taxable asset of immense value; the mines have been levied upon freely. The local residents seldom objected to tax rates because the taxes they paid individually were increased tenfold by mining tax revenues.

Thus, residents of the Range find the lavish spending of tax moneys for the public weal perfectly natural. The individual who has wealth seldom lives as though he were a pauper: Why should the town with wealth live as though it possessed little? Then there is ever present the thought expressed by an Eveleth fireman: "Why shouldn't these towns have everything they want? If we don't get it, it will go to New York to buy cigars for the damn capitalists down there. All we'll have left anyway is big holes in the ground out there." When one considers the wealth of the towns, he is surprised that they do not spend far more. Perhaps the most amazing thing of all is that with all their taxable assets the towns are frequently burdened with debt and at times are seriously embarrassed by a shortage of city funds.

Hibbing closed its first year by ordering bills totaling $1,653.99 paid. Twenty-five years later bills were totaling well over a million dollars annually. The Auditor's Report of 1929 showed a levy of $1,994,337.32 for Hibbing, yet in the year 1929, Hibbing was very embarrassed financially. The long period of conflict drove the town to spending extremes that have been incorporated in the mores of the community and in the habits and tastes of the citizenry. These practices have gathered momentum with the years, and legal restrictions have not been sufficient to change long-established habits and customs.

Eveleth is, likewise, plunging forward into annual litigation and injunctions; tax moneys are exhausted a year ahead of time; large obligations must be met by warrants. The citizens suffer for want of intelligent and conservative leadership. The mining companies have established restrictions by the per capita law, but the community is still dominated by an urge toward extravagance.

Virginia has, on the other hand, fostered a conservative policy, as mining towns go, and has not been embarrassed by legislative measures or by the depression. Her traditions of conservative management have, likewise, been cumulative and have taken on the characteristic of a cultural compulsive.

What are the differential factors in the situation?

Differential Spending

That the spending pattern in Virginia is different from that in the other Range towns is attested by varied types of evidence. First, the comparative levies of the three towns for municipal purposes may be cited. Hibbing, a village of approximately 15,000 population, has levied more than two and a quarter millions of dollars in a single year. For the last twelve years her annual levies have averaged over two millions. Eveleth, with approximately 7,000 population, levied well over a million dollars in 1920. In the twelve years since it has levied an aggregate of more than nine and a quarter millions. Virginia has a much better tax record, with an expenditure for the twelve years (1921-1932) of about seven and one quarter millions. Virginia's population has averaged approximately 13,000 for the period.

Second, a comparison of financial obligations of the three towns shows that Virginia is the most secure as far as debts are concerned. Her small bonded indebtedness is not in undesirable liabilities but is simply an extension of credit to people who have installed city heat. Hibbing and Eveleth have heavy debts, totaling almost three and one-half millions and almost a half million respectively.

A visitor to the three Range towns has difficulty in seeing a difference in services acquired through the differential expenditures. Virginia has about everything in the way of municipal and school properties that a town could wish for. They are not quite as lavish as are some Hibbing properties but are far more attractive than Eveleth properties. For years Virginia has spent much less money. The difference is explained, in part, by the fact that there is more efficient management.

Third, testimonial evidence given by Virginia residents and by those of Hibbing and Eveleth is abundant to the effect that Virginia is different in its spending pattern.

The following explanation seems reasonable, if not fully adequate:

Virginia is not a typical mining town. Up to 1931, she had lumber mills which provided work for 1,300 men and a substantial tax income. Moreover, taxable iron resources within the limits of the city are relatively much smaller than for either Hibbing or Eveleth. Hibbing's total valuation has exceeded $90,000,000, Eveleth's $18,000,000, whereas Virginia's valuation has at no time exceeded

$21,000,000.[12] Virginia has been approximately equal in size with Hibbing and about twice as large as Eveleth.

There is another significant difference. Local residents in Virginia have paid approximately 30 percent of their taxes, whereas in Eveleth about 92 percent and in Hibbing about 95 percent have been paid by mining companies. [13]

These combined differences, each of which helps explain the other, cover a multitude of differences in spending habits. Virginia residents have had vested interests in keeping expenditures within the bounds of reason. Approximately a third of the money being spent was their money. They have elected and reelected men whom they could trust to preserve their conservative traditions. There has also been the factor of conflict in local politics, which may have been largely accidental in its origin, but which has been perpetuated through the years. Previous to 1912 it centered in vice policies. Subsequent to that time for a long period it centered in the question of the ownership of public utilities. There have been no major policies of difference since 1920, but the dissension continues. Conflict within has hindered the unifying of public forces against the mining company; this has been a blessing in disguise. Then the continuous clerkship of Alford Ford has probably been an important factor in keeping affairs going straight.[14] Ford has kept books while other city clerks have manipulated records to gain desired ends. [15]

The Hibbing and Eveleth publics have been united against the mining companies. Mayors and councils have worked together to get the most possible from public office. All the citizens asked was a beneficient paternalism. For every dollar the citizens paid in taxes the absentee owner paid between $90.00 and $95.00.

Footnotes for chapter X

1. Schedule 2, Report of Public Examiner, 1916.

2. In an interview with the writer.

3. Minnesota Yearbook, 1921, pp. 212-218.

4. Ibid.

5. Ms. of 163 pp., on file in Office of State Public Examiner, St. Paul.

6. Exhibit "C" of Mining Companies Report to State Tax Commission; See 1930 Report State Tax Commission.

7. Statement made to the writer in an interview, 1932.

8. The cutting remarks of the State Public Examiner, in his report on the affairs in Hibbing, prepared in 1922, is suggestive of conditions. The report is on file in the St. Paul office of the State Public Examiner.

9 See typed reports of the State Public examiner on file in the St. Paul office.

10. Ibid.

11. Ibid.

12. State Auditor's Report.

13. Typewritten statement furnished by an Oliver Iron Mining Company official.

14. The Public Examiner complimented Mr. Ford for his efficient records in the only public examination the city has had; op. cit.

15. See Public Examiners Reports for Hibbing and Eveleth, op. cit.

Chapter XI

THE EVOLUTION OF THE ORE TAXATION POLICY

The tax complex is always a vital one in any community but is exceedingly important in an iron-mining municipality. This is true both when it involves the assessments on personal real estate and private property and when it involves assessments on corporation property and mineral resources. Fundamentally, the Range towns have faced two problems: the first, that of insuring a sufficient local income from mining properties; the second, that of shielding the mining companies from excessive taxation by the State. In reality these problems have been one and the same. The matter of shielding the mining companies from state taxes has not grown out of any benevolent disposition on the part of the municipalities toward the mining companies, but out of a feeling that if more of the tax goes to the State the smaller will be the share of the local community. The State, on the other hand, is faced with the problem of preserving for the commonwealth a share of its natural heritage in iron ore through tax revenues. The mining companies are interested in the reduction of taxes with a consequent increase in profits.

Participation of Range Towns in Taxation Developments

In pioneer times little thought was given to taxation either by the local communities or by the State. Later the tax issue became a vital one in which three groups were interested, the mining companies, the State, and the Range towns. These groups have participated in a triangular conflict which has led to the present policy of taxation. In the history of the Mesabi, the towns have been allied at times with the mining companies and at other times with the State. During the period from 1906 to 1920 the State was constantly attempting to get a larger share of the taxes in

opposition to the Range municipalities, which united with
the mining companies. Since 1920 the mining companies
have been attempting to limit local taxes through the
influence of the State legislature, so the policy of the towns
has been one of self-defense against encroachments both
by mining companies and the State.

In the spring of 1915 the Harrison Bill was a live
issue. It called for a per capita limitation of expenditures in
municipalities of over 5,000 population to $25.00 per year.

At that time the mining companies circulated a
pamphlet accusing eight of the Range villages of raising
more taxes proportionately than did 140 other villages and
cities of the State. It was shown that in the 140 towns per
capita expenditures for municipal purposes averaged $5.35
annually; for Duluth $11.01; for St. Paul $11.20; and for
Minneapolis $12.52; whereas for Hibbing it was almost
$100.00 per capita, or $500.00 for each family of five.
Hibbing at this time had a population of approximately
12,000, and during the year 1914 spent approximately
$1,200,000 (excluding school expenditures)--more than the
entire general levy of Duluth, a city seven times larger. In
spite of this high levy, Hibbing's indebtedness had increased
from $284,792 in January 31, 1913 to $1,252,597, in
January 31, 1915. For the previous ten years taxes in
Hibbing had increased about twenty-seven times as fast
as had the population. The mining companies were paying
98 percent of the taxes. The same general story applied
to several other Range towns, namely Chisholm, Buhl,
Keowatin, and Mountain Iron.

The Range people had another story. They appealed
to the legislature to protect them against the aggression of
the "millionaire mine owners of the East." In the Hibbing
Tribune of April 17, 1915 the arguments published were:

Don't Forget: That Hibbing is an island,
surrounded by yawning open pits and underlaid by iron ore--you can stand in the center of

the business district of Hibbing and almost
throw a baseball into four of the biggest open
iron ore pits in the world--and mining operations account for by far the greater portion of
Hibbing's expenditures. There has never been a
year when Mining Companies were in control
of Hibbing that they did not spend more the
$25.00 per capita. Don't Forget: That the
Mining Companies have bought men and newspapers and village councils from the Range to
testify that this bill is fair--every one of which
men or newspapers or councils are either mining officials or deeply involved with the Mining
Companies. Don't Forget: That the Mining
Companies say, "The per capita limit will affect
only villages and cities on the Ranges"--
neglecting to tell you that other parts of the bill
will affect the bonding and taxing powers of
every village and city in the state. [1]

Seabold was given most of the credit for having
defeated the Harrison Bill. He was called "the Napoleon of
Hibbing." On his return at 10:56 p.m., on the twenty-second
of April, he was met by a band, and a crowd with torchlights
and fireworks. The celebration lasted until morning. He
was given a big banquet in Hibbing, and his friends at that
time suggested that he run for the governorship. This fight
also proved a great publicity stunt for Hibbing. Announce-
ments of her white way and lavish municipal expenditures
were publicized throughout the nation.

Range attitudes on the local tax question are well
expressed in the <u>Mesabi Ore</u> of Hibbing.

The "Ore" believes that every cent
possible should be collected from the mining
companies while they are with us, to the end
that we may retain unto ourselves a share of
the wealth that, once removed, will never
return....we do not believe in waste or extrava-

gance in municipal management or anywhere
else, but we shall hold that Hibbing should collect every year the one and one-half million
dollars due it from the mining companies.

We owe it to ourselves to collect every
cent available from the taxation of these mines
and use it to beautify our towns because it
belongs to us. Hibbing surely receives no
thanks for handing over a million dollars a
year of its own money to Eastern mine owners,
and we will be just as well treated if we collect
and spend all that is due us.[2]

Range citizens again sent hundreds of wires to the
governor protesting the per capita tax limitation law in
1921, which called for the reduction of municipal expenditures to $50.00 per person. They succeeded in raising the
requirements to $100.00. Despite their later attempts to
have the law repealed, it continued in force and was revised
in 1929 calling for the following scale: 1929, $100.00 per
capita; 1930, 1931, $80.00; 1932, $75.00; 1933, and thereafter $70.00. Since 1929 the towns have been concerned
with the problem of keeping expenditures within the law.

Increasing Municipal Valuations by the Annexation of Ore Properties

A device for increasing tax assessments frequently
resorted to in Range towns has been that of annexing
mining properties, so that they could be covered by city
tax assessments.

A few instances will illustrate that this has not been
an infrequent procedure. In 1905 districts northwest and
south of Virginia voted themselves into the corporate limits
of the city. This move, led by the Virginia citizens doubled
the assessed valuation of their town.

A news item in the Virginia <u>Enterprise</u> of January 29, 1909, states the attitude of the Range citizens toward annexation:

> The taking in by annexation all the property that was voted into the city limits in November, 1905 was the greatest "stunt" ever pulled off in this city, although but few taxpayers realized what a fight there was by a handful of citizens to accomplish it. It meant an increase in the real-estate valuation of the city of eight and one-half millions of dollars--that's all.

Even though Hibbing has annexed several properties, her annexation problem has no doubt been a less vital one than that of the other Range towns. Hibbing has remained a village, even though exceeding 15,000 population. This means that she has spent a large part of the taxes of the Township of Stunts. She has virtually all the surrounding mining locations with her reach for a limited amount of taxation.

The Evolution of State Taxation Policy

There is little question but that the Minnesota policy of ore taxation in the early days was far too lenient for the good of the state. Taxes have been increased through the years until many groups feel that they are now too heavy for the good of the mining industry. The combined taxes upon the ore-mining industry have provided an annual state revenue running beyond the twenty million mark.

Every tax measure favoring the State has been gained in the face of paid lobbyists, working for the mining industry, and opposition from the Range towns. These measures have been maintained only by rejecting company appeals for lowered taxation. An extensive appeal was made to the State Tax Commission and appears in their

1928 report. It was signed by sixteen mining companies and presented evidence to show that the best interests of the State were to be attained through lowered taxes, thus preserving the mining industry and aiding its development of low-grade ores. We are not interested in evaluating the state taxation policy, but simply in pointing out the role of conflict in the evolution of the system now in existence.

An Analysis of the Factors in the Evolution of the Ore Taxation Policy

Ore taxes at the present time are distributed in Minnesota as follows:[3]

Taxes	Percent State	Percent County and Municipality	Percent Trust Fund
Ad Valorem	10.5	69.5	-
Occupation	50	-	50
Royalty	100	-	-

Previous to 1921, the great bulk of the taxes went to the local communities. Even at the present time approximately three-fourths of iron ore taxes go to county and local governments, since ad valorem revenues are by far the largest.

Previous to 1912, the State was getting less than a million dollars in ore taxes by which the local communities on the Range were almost entirely supported. However, the mining communities had been able to maintain favorable south state opinion, and there was little desire on the part of legislatures to interfere with the welfare of the infant villages or with the new industry. The messages to the legislators and governors from the Range communities and from the mining companies were effective. Moreover, the State had not learned to depend upon mineral income. The mining companies and local communities worked together

harmoniously, and the State was not considered an enemy
to either, except at times when moves were made by certain
groups in the legislature to increase ore taxes.

After the conflict developed between the Range
towns and the mining companies, news of public extravagance began to filter into sections of the State beyond the
Range. The Range towns publicized their prosperity; they
sought notoriety and fame through public display.
Moreover, the mining companies called attention of legislators to the extravagance of the towns; gossip circulated
widely about million dollar schools with gold doorknobs,
and of libraries with Persian rugs on the floors. Many similar stories, composed of fact and fiction, were noised abroad.

The Range towns' use of tax money could not but
bring an unfavorable reaction. Legislatures, composed
largely of non-range residents, would not stand by and see
funds, to which they felt the commonwealth had a right,
squandered. A perishable heritage was the right of the
State. Consequently, there followed the legislation already
described, increasing State taxes and reducing local tax
power. About 1922, Hibbing began to realize where the
publicity that had been circulated was leading and turned
about face. Since then it has been a Hibbing policy to hinder
publicity that might create attitudes unfavorable to the
Range.

The mining companies have made little net gain in
the triangular struggle with local communities and the
State. They have bridled the local communities quite successfully by the per capita law, but additional state taxes
that were added at the same time local expenditures were
limited have absorbed what was gained through the limitation of local taxation. Their future attack will doubtless be
focused upon reduced state taxation. The Range towns
themselves have little to hope for in the way of increased
taxation privileges. They have overstepped both with the
mining companies and with the state legislatures.

Footnotes for chapter XI

1. April 17, 1915.

2. For a discussion of the various tax measures see the following reports of the Minnesota Tax Commission, 1928, chs. VIII-X, ch. 5.

3. Purdee, J. S., <u>The Children's Heritage</u>.

Chapter XII

THE DEVELOPMENT OF THE POLITICAL MORES

Government of the three Range towns are and always have been normal in their form of organization. They are far from normal, however, in governmental mores. The expedient policy has been practiced widely. The mores have been characterized by a willingness to overlook any violation of standard codes that would bring public or private gain at the expense of the mining interests.

The philosophy of patronage has permeated the thinking of the masses, and people have come to expect that their personal needs and desires will be gratified through those in public office. The widespread practice of a paternalistic policy by politicians has created a group-wide sense of dependence upon public resources, even at the expense of individual initiative and enterprise.

The mores of a community are objectified in its accepted policies and practices. We will first try to learn what the community mores are and then attempt to explain their appearance and widespread acceptance.

What Are the Political Mores?

Spending versus Economy: Until recent years economy has not been a campaign issue in politics. "The full dinner-pail," "Seabold, Prosperity, Progress," and such slogans have been the keynote. In Chapters IX and X the spending pattern has been described. Extravagant spending has had the full sanction of the local communities.

Political Consciousness: "Everything is politics on the Range," is an expression one frequently encounters, and one need not be on the Range long to become convinced of its truth. "In Southern Minnesota, it means nothing to be on the school board or in city office. Here it means everything," said a Range social worker. A minister emphatically declared: "Politics is the curse of the Range." Immediately upon entering the boundaries of St. Louis County, one observes large signs "Vote for X for Commissioner," "Vote for Z for Commissioner," etc., along all highways. Later the observer learns that these signs have been prepared and erected by paving contractors who have vested interests in getting their candidate elected.

Sooner or later any climber in economic or social life must reckon with the grim realities of politics. The basic interest seems to by personal gain and the obtaining of jobs for friends. Even men who have higher motives are credited with graft and patronage by the public.

The Spoils System: In practically all fields of government, offices and jobs are subject to the hazards of political appointment, as every change in major political offices means a change in a large group of appointive officers and workmen. The political mores have long sanctioned this policy, and it is only recently that there is any tendency to eliminate it, even in those departments where frequent changes are hazardous to public safety, namely, police and fire departments. The spoils system extends not only to appointive offices, but to common labor. Whether or not one's "side" is in has made a lot of difference.

A newly-elected council in Virginia in 1932 dismissed all street and public building employees and appointed its own men in their stead. In Hibbing the hazards of political jobs were illustrated by a recent change in the school board, which was followed by a wholesale dismissal of employees.

The spoils system mores have changed, after years of agitation, concerning protective officers. Police and firemen of Eveleth and Hibbing have recently been put on a civil service basis.

Paternalism: Paternalism has for years been incorporated in the political mores. It has taken two main forms, subsidizing business and subsidizing labor. The one, that of aiding business enterprises by patronage of the city, is clearly indicated by testimonial evidence and by extensive records in the official reports of the State Public Examiner.

The second form of paternalism is that of hiring labor from public funds to a degree altogether out of proportion to the villages' needs for labor. The Public Examiner's report for Hibbing in 1916 indicated that during the year 1914, when 1,178 votes were cast for mayor, there were as many as 1,011 men on the monthly payroll. During 1915, when there were 1,710 votes, the number of men on the payroll was as high as 1,296. Paying salaries, when no work was done, paying telephone charges for private phones from city funds, and other violations are cited.

Public parasitism has been exhibited in numerous lawsuits directed against the city. It is also present in the public relief system. The effects in blighting individual initiative have been realized to a considerable degree. In the words of an Eveleth schoolman, "Everyone born in this town feels that the city owes him a living just because he was born here."

Local newspaper accounts tell of large numbers of lawsuits aimed at collecting funds from the public treasury. We are not here concerned with the justice or injustice of the many claims which have annually come to the attention of the officials. It is a rather interesting reflection on a community's attitude, since claims of this nature are so frequently presented with no comeback of adverse public opinion from the taxpayers. People with real or alleged injuries have been greatly encouraged in presenting claims by the fact that many of them were paid willingly by the communities. The recent tax limitations imposed by the legislature has curbed the liberal policy of city officials during the last few years, and many claims have been rejected.

The mining companies have also been defendant
in many suits. The village and private parties have tried
again and again to recover funds from the mining interests.

The problem of providing for the poor in the three
Iron Range towns has been solved by work relief. Since dole
were given by Carnegie in the nineties, comparatively little
direct relief was given until the depression of the thirties.
The method of relief has been that of city employment. The
tax incomes have usually made it possible to expand the
payroll to almost any proportions, because legitimate
expenditures have been the extent of the administration's
use of money. When needless extravagance and waste have
crept in, tax incomes have been devoured, and crises have
found the cities faced with the necessity of cutting the payroll. A depression instance is to the point. Eveleth had to cut
her city payroll mercilessly in 1933 and had to depend upon
the schools to carry the heavy load of employment. With
wise expenditures during the depression years citizens of
Eveleth would have been able to expand the payroll to meet
the exigencies of the situation. "If the damn politicians
hadn't grafted so much they could carry some of the people
now like the schools are doing. The schools, you know, are
rich and can carry a lot of people," was the indictment of a
Eveleth merchant.

Virginia, with much less mining tax income, employed men extensively during this period of depression.
The situation is summarized in a statement by a city
official:

> Our payroll in common labor has
> jumped from $4,000 per month to $16,000 per
> month, and still everything is paid for. Every
> man who is employed by the city is working.
> We are employing on the average of 600 men
> per month, two weeks at a time.

Excessive taxation and the squandering of funds has
at times been defended by arguments relating to the sea

sonal nature of mine employment and to the necessity of maintaining the unemployed workers by city "jobs." Politicians have frequently been unscrupulous in stimulating the development of this attitude, and in making the most of it for selfish political gains. Many times the need for city labor has been a subterfuge rather than a reality.

Even "jobs" as a form of relief have produced a mild form of pauperization. It has fostered a spirit of dependence upon public funds. People have developed the attitude that the city and schools owe them a livelihood. Many request work who would never expect or accept outright charity. This imposes an expenditure on the city treasury that probably only a mining community could bear.

Graft: Rumors are current of the widespread practice of graft in the Range towns. The reaction of the voters and juries to exposures of graft indicates that the majority of them have taken it for granted. Everywhere on the Range, as well as outside, one hears of Range graft. The most conclusive evidence is found in the Public Examiner's Reports.

Virginia is not to be included in the discussion of paternalistic and graft mores. This is because there is no tangible evidence of such practice in the city.

Factors in the Development of the Political Mores

Politicians: The politician has played a dominant role in the towns with a heterogeneous immigrant population. Hibbing and Eveleth each have such a population, and each have produced leaders who were master politicians. A mining company official expressed it thus:

When it comes to being led into politics, these foreigners are led into everything by some prominent American. They are honest, but are easily influenced.

Victor Seabold, president of Hibbing, was no doubt the most successful politician that ever raised his head in the Range country. He understood the common man's psychology. He knew the value of a slogan, of giving aid to the poor families, of being interested in humanitarian enterprises, and of playing up the stereotype that was the common object of hatred--"the Capitalistic Steel Corporation." "The full dinner-pail" slogan seldom fails to make an appeal to the masses, and especially when this program is carried out after election. He was the super-man, idealized by all the immigrant working men. "Vic said" put a stamp of finality on any issue.

His knowledge of human psychology is also shown by the fact that he seldom lost a court case as a lawyer. He could win when everything apparently was against his side of the case.

As a politician Seabold knew how to build his machine and keep it intact. In order to hold the business men he threatened to fire any man from the city payroll who was known to order from a mail-order house; to hold the workers, all unemployed were put on the city payroll. His political enemies were shown to be identified with the mining interests. The mining interests were the offspring of "eastern capitalists" who were preying on the workers and at the same time removing the wealth from their community. Spectacular trials with the mining companies in which he upheld the injured or those who suffered property damages, kept him ever in the limelight then there were the visits to the legislature to lobby for laws favoring the Range municipalities. At all times the building of great public works for his own Hibbing, consultations with experts and similar activities, kept Seabold and Hibbing before the outside public. Naturally Hibbing could not be thought of without thinking of Seabold.

Victor Seabold has been dead since the year 1926; he lives only in memory now. Yet one cannot broach the subject of politics among Range people in any of the towns without having these memories revived.

Victor Camack, the present mayor of Eveleth, has been in that office for ten years. His praises and curses are far flung throughout the city itself and among the mining officials in adjoining cities. His ability to escape the clutches of the law in the face of accusations and litigation over supposed misuse of city funds testify to his ability to handle the law. Whatever else he may or may not be, he is a skillful politician.

In Virginia one man has acted as city clerk for thirty-seven years. He has kept records that have been above reproach and has doubtless been an important influence in keeping many vicious practices out of government.

<u>Nationality Groups</u>: "The only purpose of Nationality Organizations on the Range is political--to get jobs." This expresses strongly the place of nationalities in politics. "In Eveleth," says a minister, "people talk of nationalities in terms of votes. There are 250 Italian votes, 300 Austrian votes, 1,000 Slovanian votes, etc."

Great stress is placed on the voting right of the foreign population, and "I'll tell the world they vote." Foreigners covet the privilege of voting, as this is the one road to the "jobs" politicians give in return for the support. Americanization seems to have been given a political cast.

<u>Vocational Insecurity</u>: Vocational insecurity has given a long arm to the vote, causing the native born to be no less interested in proper political affiliations than is the foreigner. "Job consciousness" has been awakened by the scarcity of "jobs." "There's no work," is the comment of almost every laborer. The merchants echo the sentiment, for no work means store bills and poor business. The politicians respond to the situation with made "jobs." The "job" has been a dominant problem since the 1921 depression. Since 1930 it has been the almost universal quest on the Range. Public employment has been the only hope, and this

hope is identified with the right use of political influence and of the ballot. As was suggested by one mother, the wife of a working man: "Politics is awful. If you say anything you get in bad, and if you don't say anything you get in bad. It's getting so you can't get any work unless you're in politics."

Mining companies have also influenced the vote at times, having urged their employees to vote for candidates that favored the company's interests. The mining company affiliation of candidates for office seem to be a major issue in most elections.

The voting interest seems to center basically about the employment issue. The politician who can promise the most jobs is likely to carry the election. The vote is the only thing the immigrant has to sell to the politician for his favors. In case the mining company is in control of politics, it is safer to sell the vote there.

<u>Religious Groups</u>: An undercurrent of religious sentiment is reflected in politics. While candidates do not campaign on the basis of religion, it is generally known that the religious persuasion of the candidate, or of his wife, is an influential factor in either a municipal or school election.

There were seventeen candidates for office in a recent aldermanic race in Virginia, fifteen Protestants and two Catholics. A minister expressing his sentiments on the outcome of the campaign said, "The Protestants won, thank God!"

A man's religion makes a difference in getting votes. In fact, the wife's religion may be a decided factor with some. "Many Protestants did not vote for Jones because his wife was a Catholic," suggested an Eveleth voter.

The Ku Klux Klan played an important part in politics after the World War period. Because of the secret nature of the operations of this organization, it is difficult to say just what were the consequences of its activities. In Virginia especially, this group fostered an anti-Catholic spirit that is still felt in both school and municipal elections. In Hibbing the Klan has about ceased activities.

Absentee Ownership: Mining, as the basic industry, has paid the larger proportion of the taxes in all the Range towns. The attitude of a politician toward the mining companies is an important factor in his administration. If he is in sympathy with the mining interests, it is assumed that he will be conservative in spending, and will cry to foster a spirit of good will between them and the town. If, on the other hand, he is directly opposed to the mining companies, it is assumed that he will get the most that can be gotten for the people through tax levies. In each of the towns the mining company and labor factions have had their "ins" and "outs" in office.

Hibbing has had non-mining company presidents almost constantly since 1913. Eveleth has been in the control of non-company men for several years. This particular issue in Virginia politics has been a much less active one because the town has always been more conservative in its spending.

Mining towns are abnormal in the sense that the major taxpayer is not a member of the community and has little or no control over local government. In such a setting it is difficult to keep paternalism out of government, and when it once gets in it is very difficult to eradicate.

The masses have developed a hatred for "Eastern Capitalists" and for the "Steel Trust." Just how their stereotypes have been formed one can scarcely tell. It seems, however, that politicians, in seeking outside foes upon which to center the attention of the masses in order to escape the scrutiny their own behavior has merited, have purposely created them. The people have generally had a favorable attitude toward the local mining company superintendents and captains, but they hate the capitalists "down in New York City and Philadelphia." The fact that most of the workers for the Oliver Company are stockholders of the Steel Trust is never called to their attention. The "Steel Trust" stereotype probably has no counterpart in reality. The stereotype is none the less real, and the conflict between the local residents and the Steel Trust is none the less intense.

Local Traditions: As culture grows in any area over a period of history the accumulative experiences of the culture building group take on the nature of cultural compulsives, in that uniformity in attitudes develops in the common cultural mould. This similarity in idealogy directs cultural change toward certain designed ends or in the quest of certain desired values that the group has come to appreciate. On the mental side these compulsives may be thought of as patterns that have become, through interaction, the possession of most individuals in the group. They have continuity in the group and frequently express themselves in concerted action, leaving no doubt as to their meaning.

Virginia has fostered a tradition that keeps it free from paternalistic policy. Public utilities are municipally owned, but all customers are charged for them. The installation of public utilities and monthly rentals are and have been on a purely business basis. The people are satisfied to pay a reasonable sum for their utilities and to work for the city, putting in a day at labor, generally speaking.

Victor Seabold introduced the paternalistic policy into Hibbing government on a wholesale scale. It carries over to the present time to a great degree. Extravagances in city luxuries are taken as a matter of course. The "full dinner pail" came to mean a dinner pail filled by tax moneys.

Camack's mayorship developed a paternalistic policy in Eveleth. Many soon accepted it as the order of the day and profited by it when they could do so. Those traditions acted as compulsives.

Since the enactment of the per capita law, increasing numbers in Hibbing and Eveleth have become interested in greater municipal thrift, yet the old drives, resident in individual habit and group tradition, tend to persist. Thus creating new compulsives is as difficult as is the obliterating of old ones.

Summary

What then are the factors that have meant the most in the evolution of the local political mores? Absentee ownership of taxable resources, large expenditures to be made by politicians, and unscrupulous leadership preying upon religious prejudices and immigrant ignorance.

Chapter XIII

LAGS IN GROUP ADJUSTMENT

We have studied in some detail the relationships between the public and the mining companies. We are primarily concerned in this chapter with the relationships existing between the laborers and the mining companies. The gap between the two groups has widened through the years. The lag in adjustment between the laborers and the employers is a product of numerous conflicts that have marked the history of these groups on the Mesabi. Tardy adjustments of conflicting issues have intensified antagonism and thus prepared the way for more bitter conflicts as new difficulties have appeared. The accumulative effect of these tardy adjustments has been to develop permanent antagonisms.

Regions of Strain in Mining Company Labor Relations

Basic to an understanding of mining company-labor relations is the problem of the machine as it has affected employment.

Mining technology has improved each year, resulting in fewer jobs and more unemployment. Practically every improvement in machine technique has worked a hardship on some group of mine employees. This difficulty has been progressively accumulative. Let us turn to some instances.

The evolution of the machine as it has affected labor can be very clearly seen in the development of open-pit mining methods on the Mesabi. When the first open-pits were mined, loading was done with the hand shovel and with chutes built into the slopes of the pit. The dump cars were crude affairs, made entirely of wood, with a capacity of only six or seven tons, and drawn by mules.

105

Then came the light steam engine, which could draw a longer train of cars. About 1892, the first steam shovel was introduced into the Range at Biwabik.

The electric shovel was introduced about 1923. After a brief trial, it was found so satisfactory that it replaced practically all the steam shovels. The electric shovels were mounted on caterpillar wheels so did not require the laying of track. They had larger dippers, with a five-yard capacity.

Of course, similar improvements in technique have been made in every phase of mining--in handling ore at the docks, stock piles, and laboratories, as well as work in the machine shops. Electric locomotives have made their appearance, as well as have automatic switches, doing away with the locomotive firemen and switchmen. In 1910, the mines were producing 1,522 tons of ore for every man employed; in 1920, they produced 2,651 tons, and in 1930, 4,257 tons. [1]

While these figures indicate clearly that more ore is being produced per man, the coming of more efficient machines made, for a time, more permanent labor conditions. In the early days of open pit mining the work was seasonal; as better machines were developed winter was no obstacle to operations, so the work of stripping and of piling ore in stock piles continued through the winter months, even though the lakes were not open for shipment.

But this tremendous increase in production due to modern machinery has made it possible for the mines to supply the ore demands of the furnaces in a very short time. Whereas the mines once had to run at capacity the entire shipping season, now they run only a few months to supply the demand. The large five-yard shovels employed in the last decade have uncovered enough ore so that very little stripping is necessary. This has brought about the periodic closing of operations for the winter months.

The mine laborer, confronted with the question of present unemployment conditions, invariably attributes his state to the development of the machine.

It is quite clear from this brief summary of cultural growth in technology that: First, material culture has accumulated with great rapidity, the new and better devices having been added and older machines having been discarded; second, and what is more important in this connection, adjustments in group relations have in no way kept pace. The mining companies have been motivated by profits, and machine technique has been improved at the cost of the workingman's job. The mining companies have taken the position that the laborer's welfare was not a matter with which they should concern themselves, or at least that it was secondary to profits. The laborer has, in turn, become cynical regarding the machine and increasingly hostile in his attitude toward the mining companies.

A second region of strain has been the issues raised by fanatical labor agitators or by organized labor groups. These issues have led to open conflict, for each labor strike, if it originates in and is supported widely by local unions, is the result of the accumulation of unsettled issues between employer and employee. Let us briefly review the labor situation on the Mesabi.

Labor organizations as such never have flourished on the Range. Immigrants, unaccustomed to American ways and unable to speak the American language, have constituted a large part of the mining population. The recent immigrant provided poor material out of which to weld an organization that could in any way match strength and wits against the United States Steel and other great corporations whose subsidiaries mine the ores of the Mesabi. Strike leaders have been raw immigrants. Americans and Anglo-Saxon immigrants have held the responsible positions in mining and have had satisfactory incomes, so they have not been given to labor agitation.

The Range miners have had their conflicts with
employers, notwithstanding. It is perhaps of little significance that the labor group always lost. This was to be
expected in the nature of things as they existed on the
Range. Labor's struggles were spasmodic outbursts, often
made unwisely. They did not necessarily grow out of deep
felt grievances or aim at reasonable ends; they were the
product of selfish leaders who, through agitation for selfish
gains, unionized the workers for the period and won their
ends. Not that labor has not had its grievances in mining.
They have had them, and in cases the strike has helped to
air them and has indirectly brought some corrections in
working conditions which have been of far-reaching
importance.

There have been three strikes of some consequence
on the Mesabi Range.[2] The first was in the middle
nineties, when mining companies had little use for labor
due to the widespread panic throughout the country; they
almost welcomed the strike. At such a time it could but fail.

The second strike was better timed.[3] The way had
been prepared by a year's sowing of discontent among workers by members of the Western Federation of Labor. It
broke on July 25, 1907, during the time of the dock worker's
strike at the lake ports. Although the time was opportune
for labor to make some gains, the character of leadership
and following brought it to failure. A list of the names of its
leaders is suggestive of their recency in America. Teofile
Petriella (Italian Socialist), H. di Stofane, Oscar
Luihlumen, Aate Heiskemon, C. Anderson, J. Maki, John
Kolu, A. Takela, Frank Lucas, John Movern, R. Lundstrom,
E. McHale, F. Menarind, and J. Connors. These men were
representatives of the Western Federation of Miners, under
the general supervision of Bill Haywood, but as leaders they
failed to inspire the sympathies of the Range communities
toward the movement. The merchants refused credit to the
strikers, and openly confessed their sympathy with the mining companies.

The Finns, with their stubborn determination, held out to the last. Southern Europeans were shipped in to replace them. At one time in August they came 600 strong-- Montenegrins, Bulgarians, Servians, and Greeks. When the strike was finally broken, the mining companies refused to employ Finns who had participated in the Strike. This had far-reaching consequences to St. Louis County and to the Range. Thousands of the Finns went into the rural districts and developed farms. The present state of development of the hinterland of the Range towns is largely an outgrowth of this labor crisis.

This exodus of the Finns from the Range towns and their replacement by Southern Europeans did much to change the nationality complexion of the Range, as well as to erect a barrier of animosity between Finns and the mining companies.

The third and final great struggle of labor came in 1916, under the leadership of the International Workers of the World. Briefly, the strike issues were the following: The miners wanted $2.75 per day for open-pit mining, $3.00 per day for underground dry work and $3.50 for underground work. They wanted an eight-hour day for all, pay twice a month, and the abolition of the contract system.

The strike leaders of 1907 were the strikers of 1916, and their sacrifices for the cause of labor were as futile as were those of the earlier groups.

Workers have been disillusioned regarding the merits of unions, and some have lost faith in the ability of the workers to successfully band together for a common end. Now that hard times have come, the strike is a useless weapon.

This lack of open resistance, then, does not indicate amicable relations, so much as it does hopelessness on the part of labor. Theirs is a passive resistance that grows out of past failure and a feeling that the odds are overwhelm ing, should open resistance be made. While this is a more peaceful method than strikes and lockouts, one wonders if such a state of mind is as healthful as the hope of gains through staging open and successful resistance.

A third region of strain in labor-industry relations has centered in the employment issue. No other issue has been so productive of animosity toward the mining companies. Idle men brood over their plight and blame the group that produced it.

Public Sympathy with Labor

The sympathy of the Range public, for the most part, is with the laboring man. Merchants and the professions have vested interests in the wages laborers receive, but the interest probably runs much deeper. Community prosperity is inevitably tied up with the prosperity of the working man.

"Business is bad," was the comment of a Virginia grocer in 1932. "Before we had to carry accounts a long time. Now we don't know how long. Bad before. Worse now."

Community Spending, The Region of Strain in Public-Mining Company Relations

It has already been clearly indicated by evidence presented in Chapter X that the chief region of strain in mining company-government relations has been the matter of public expenditures. Further explanation of the spending pattern in relation to industry is desirable.

The great corporations which replaced most of the independent companies that took possession of the Mesabi around 1900 had only one aim--profits for stockholders. They introduced a predatory pattern in dealing with the employees and with the State's heritage in ore. The foregoing survey of the relations between labor and industry suggest this pattern. The public gradually sided with labor in their sympathies, and the two groups together, through controlling government, gradually adopted the same predatory pattern presented by the mining companies. Their only weapon was taxation. Through taxation they could acquire not only poor relief for labor but subsidies for struggling business enterprises; not only necessary conveniences for the public good, but luxuries. They found, through taxation, a way to reinstate beauty where industry had marred it, a way to bring culture and refinement in a locality where many nations had been mixed in a struggle for bread, a way to bring recreation and play to both unemployed youth and adults.

No attempt is made here to justify either group in this struggle; the aim is simply to try to explain existing relationships and attitudes.

In fairness to the mining companies it should be said that many local superintendents have been men of irreproachable character and of great human sympathy. It is not these men that laboring groups and public have hated but the organizations they have represented. They have liked Fry and Tully, their local superintendents, but have hated "them damned capitalists down east." The local representatives were not, however, able to meet the needs of the local situation because of the system in which they were enmeshed.

Many humanitarian enterprises have been developed by the companies, such as the employment of local social workers to distribute relief, the establishment of pensions, the beautification of company homes, the provision of a few days work per month at a time when it would have been more profitable to close the mines entirely, and the provision in recent years for a mutual welfare committee to keep in close touch with employees.

In final analysis, it is not a matter of placing blame; it is a matter of recognizing that a fundamental lag exists in adjusting relations between industry, labor, and public. Industry is probably in the best position to take the initiative, but adjustments in human relations come much harder than does the development of industrial technology. The basic maladjustment underlying conflict on the Range is not unlike that which pervades our industrial civilization.

In conclusion, we may say first, that lags in certain phases of culture produce and then perpetuate maladjustments in group relations, which group differences lead to the creation of adaptive culture designed to heal the wounds in group relations. However, it usually comes so tardily that it does not completely heal the wounds. Consequently, new conflict issues break forth calling for further adoptive culture. In final analysis, group frictions arise over values such as profits and lavish material culture, which the culture pattern has created. Group friction leads to the establishment of adaptive culture through invention or borrowing. In no case is group friction mitigated completely by the adaptive culture, for its coming is so long delayed that animosities tend to control group relations.

Footnotes for chapter XIII

1. Calculated from figures on men employed and ore produced. See Minnesota <u>Mining Directory</u>, and the <u>Annual Reports of the St. Louis County Mines Inspector</u>.

2. Each strike is described in detail in Range newspaper files, as well as in the historical editions of these papers. <u>op. cits</u>.

3. Cheney, C. B., "Labor Crisis and a Governor," <u>Outlook</u>, LXXXIX, 24-30

PART IV

AN ANALYSIS OF CULTURAL CHANGE

Chapter XIV

THE ROLE OF THE GREAT MAN IN CULTURAL CHANGE

The fiction, folklore, and drama of the mining town and frontier is vividly colored with characters who dominate the life of the pre-legal period of settlement. Their influence too carries over into the early legal period during which the revolver is more powerful than the law. These dominating characters are powerful men who master by brute force or by unusual skill or daring with weapons, and masculine women who acquire greatness by violating all the finer traditions that both men and women in a more civilized society consider essential to the female sex. The Frontier puts a premium on those with strong physical powers, who are able to survive the rigors of the natural setting, and those with elastic moral sense who can tolerate, if not condone the non-moral order which necessarily exists when highly civilized men sink to a primitive plane.

Hardly sufficient evidence exists concerning characters in the early history of the Mesabi to make any generalization with regard to the great men of the period. No one character stands out for having molded the trend of cultural development or having exercised the strong arm in social regulation. It was not until the Range became more settled and conflict between mining companies and local populations began to develop that great men who wielded a dominant influence stood out in civil affairs.

During the early period of industrialization of the Range and soon after the great corporations had assumed leadership, one man in Hibbing was influential enough so that it can be said that he influenced cultural development in a given direction. Mayor Ray was in office for several years. He was an Oliver Mining Company sympathizer and therefore tended to impose the mining company attitudes on the political structure. He and his councilmen kept the expenditures of the village low. However, public improvements were neglected. Board and cinder sidewalks, crowded school houses, and unlighted streets were symbols of the rigid economy which characterized village life. This pattern led to a violent reaction during the conflict period.

During the conflict period, also, as we have seen, one man stands out as a dominant figure, not only in carrying forward the conflict, but also in determining the type of cultural development, Victor Seabold. He defied the mining companies and rallied to his support the entire citizenry of the Range. Having done this, he transformed the culture of Hibbing from that of a primitive mining settlement to a village with a culture so extravagant that it rivaled cities five to ten times its size. For ten years he defied the mining company. With his death came the end of Hibbing supremacy, and very gradually the mining companies began to assume the position of dominance which they have since maintained with increasing effectiveness.

These observations concerning leadership on the frontier in times of conflict indicate very clearly that the "great man" is a potent factor in determining the processes of social changes as well as in determining cultural trends which characterize a given period in the history of a community. There were a number of factors which provided the necessary background in the social and cultural setting for the triumph of these men as leaders. As far as social standards were concerned, the communities were still near the frontier. The unconventional methods in politics and government which characterize the frontier were still sanctioned when these men were elected to official positions. The population of the community was composed in considerable part of a foreign element which provided a group that was readily influenced by the simple promises of the political leaders. Seabold's greatest success came while other communities beyond the Range were taking little interest in the activities of a mining community isolated in the wilderness. Had the activities of the Mesabi towns in those earlier years been scrutinized as carefully by citizens in other parts of the state and by the state legislature as they are at the present time, when the state has come to realize the potential revenue that is available through the iron deposits, it seems hardly likely that he could have so completely molded the development of the Range.

During the long conflict period in Range history another character stands in sharp contrast to the two just described, Alford Ford, city clerk of Virginia, who kept books conscientiously. He, although playing a less spectacular role, has been none the less influential. His activities, backed as they must needs have been by favorable public sentiment, have been a potent factor in determining the trend of cultural development. Whether he could have kept his office in the other two towns where the citizenry bore considerably less of their local tax burden is hard to say.

These examples indicate rather clearly one point. Leaders may play an important part in deciding which interaction process will predominate in a group at a given time. They also help keep the interaction processes uniform, so that definite interaction patterns are formed and definite trends in culture building are initiated.

Once an innovator initiates a new interaction process, and a culture trend in a given direction has resulted, both the interaction process and the culture trend help support the leader's policies and practices, whether they be of thrift or extravagance, honesty or graft. This is so much the case that their successors are expected to carry out similar policies. In fact, the attitude of public expectancy enters to enforce the interaction process and the general mores.

Chapter XV

THE LIFE CYCLE OF THE IRON-MINING TOWN

The cyclical change pattern for a total culture postulated by Chapin[1] seems to describe change in the iron-mining town according to data accumulated herein. Synchronous cycles of change in material and non-material culture are also present as underlying factors in producing the total picture of the civilization. However, this analysis of iron range culture indicates clearly that these synchronous cycles are even more pervasive than indicated in Chapin's theory; they extend to the realm of psycho-social, bio-social, and physico-social phenomena as well. Synchronous cycles on these levels, along with those on the cultural level, produce the rhythmic rise and fall of the total civilization of the mining community.

With this brief statement of the hypothesis let us review a condensed summary of evidence for rhythmic cycles of change on the levels mentioned. Let us begin first with the underlying realm of phenomena most remote from culture, the physico-social and present in order rhythmic changes in bio-social characteristics, psycho-social characteristics, and finally present rhythms in culture.

Physico-social Cycles

The first period in the history of the iron range, as far as the present culture is concerned, was occupied with the quest for, and the discovery of, ore. Preliminary investigations indicated the presence of ore, but it took a diligent search by early prospectors to locate ore bodies that could be profitably mined. When profitable bodies were located by the crude hand method, which consisted in sinking a well and windlassing out the refuse, there were the tasks of clearing forests and of building railroads to provide a way to get the ore to markets where it could be sold. The period of discovery and development was possessed of all the risks and uncertainties of a new enterprise. Fortunes that had been made in timber were drowned in ore.[2] In fact, the struggles of the nineties ended with Rockefeller in possession unexpectedly, of a large part of the developed mines and of the first railroad to the district.

Soon after 1900 the range mining enterprise was adequately financed by large corporations with permanent markets. The United States Steel, and other corporations, bought reserves to feed their furnaces for a half century ahead. With the sound financing of the mining enterprises a period of exploitation was ushered in that soon brought shipments above discoveries and hastened the range toward the depletion of high grade ore. In 1915 ore shipments exceeded discoveries as they have at all periods since.[3] The year 1913 marked the maximum remaining tonnage on the range. Since that time ore discoveries have fallen behind shipments about 18,777,000 tons annually.[4] The total shipment of ore from the Mesabi mines by decades is as follows:[5]

Period	Mesabi ore shipments - tons
1891-1900	31,389,888
1901-1910	193,495,239
1911-1920	332,924,338
1921-1930	331,953,386

The exploitation of ore has been more than exploitation in bulk. The ore of best quality has been taken first. The iron content of ore fell from 56.07 percent in 1902 to 51.19 percent in 1929.

In recent years conservation has begun. In fact, it began in earnest about 1920. At that time 35 screening and other "beneficiating" plants had been erected to improve the lower quality ore so that it could be mixed with the good ore and thus prolong the supply. Forty percent of all ore shipped in 1930 had been "beneficiated."[6] The conservation stage marks the beginning of the end. Eventually the merchantable ores of the Mesabi must disappear and with them the mining towns as such. On May 1, 1930, 43.5 percent of the merchantable ore had been mined on the Mesabi Range.[7] According to the best estimates the remaining ores will last only 20 to 30 years longer.[8] After that the most that can remain of the prosperous urban civilization of the present mining communities is small rural trade centers with meagre agricultural hinterlands.

Summarizing briefly, the physico-social cycles on the Mesabi have been first, a period of quest for and discovery of an unknown resource which spent most of its force by 1915; second, a period of wasteful exploitation of a resource that seemed inexhaustible that reached its climax just preceding 1920; third, a period of conservation of a rapidly diminishing resource which began in earnest about 1920 but which has probably not yet reached its climax. The period of serious decline in ore may be delayed for some little time, but the ore will, according to best estimates, be exhausted in approximately 20 or 30 years, thus marking the end of the mining civilization.

These fluctuations are represented graphically in the lower part of Figure II. The time span is represented on the base line and the intensity of the cycle on the vertical, the peak of the curve representing the time of its greatest intensity. The dates of the beginning and end of the cycles are only approximate since the phenomena described are of a historical nature and, therefore, are not abrupt. They are, nevertheless, periodic and can be represented approximately.

Bio-social Cycles

The mining town is characteristically a boom town

in its youth. A rapid growth to maturity, a period of relatively stable population numbers, and then a rapid decline characterize the three population growth cycles. The period of boom growth with the Mesabi towns ended soon after 1905. Previous to this time the population increased one hundred to three hundred percent each five year period. (See Table I.) Virginia in 1900 was an exception, which is explained by a fire in that year which destroyed a large part of the town. The towns made a good growth up to 1920, but since that time have remained practically stationary in population. Virginia declined approximately 15 percent in population during the decade 1920-1930.

Table I

Population of the Three Range Towns Showing Percentage Increase for Census Periods, 1895-1930*

Year	Hibbing		Virginia		Eveleth	
	Total Number	Percent Increase	Total Number	Percent Increase	Total Number	Percent Increase
1895	1,085		3,647		764	
1900	2,481	128.7	2,962	- 18.8	2,752	260.2
1905	6,566	164.7	6,056	104.5	5,332	93.8
1910	8,832	34.5	10,473	72.9	7,936	32.0
1920	15,089	70.8	14,022	33.9	7,205	2.4
1930	15,666	3.8	11,963	- 14.7	7,484	3.9

*Source: 1895 and 1905, State Census. Other years Federal Census, as the State Census was discontinued in 1905.

The mining town during its frontier stage is masculine in the extreme. The census, taken the third year after the founding of Virginia and the second year after the settlement of Hibbing and Eveleth, indicates that the ratio of males to females in Eveleth was six to one, in Hibbing five to one, and in Virginia three to one. From this extreme the trend has been gradually toward a balanced ratio. The 1930 census indicates that the sexes have about reached a balance. The number of males per 100 females for each census period was as follows:

Sex Ratio of the Three Iron Range Towns, 1895-1930

Year	1895	1905	1910	1920	1930
Hibbing	474.1	201.9	*	149.9	105.0
Virginia	271.0	190.1	169	118.5	103.4
Eveleth	600.9	177.6	*	*	107.1

The mining town is, in the beginning, a town of adults, probably consisting chiefly of young men between the ages of 20 and 40, venturesome in temperament, full of vitality and courage. Weaklings cannot survive the primitive conditions of life that must be endured during the prospecting and development period. No statistical data on age groups of the Mesabi towns are available for the first eighteen years of their history, but the opinion given is in the main correct. The second period in the history of the mining town is characterized by a youthful population. Young people with families move in and produce offspring at a high rate. On the Mesabi these groups were largely foreign, as has been true doubtless in most American mining towns. This high birth rate leads to a relatively large number in the lower age group, as is clearly indicated in Figure I which shows the relative percentage of school pupils in the various grades.[9] For the years 1895 to 1920 the primary group was abnormally large in the school population. At the same time the advanced pupils were relatively scarce.[10] As the population has aged and the birth rate has fallen, population in the primary grades has fallen markedly, and in 1930 a decreasing proportion in the intermediate grades is noted, whereas the higher grades

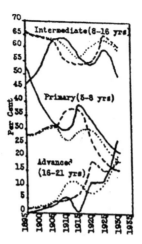

Fig. 1. Trends in School Population
in Three Mesabi Iron Range Towns, 1895-1930.
Key: Hibbing; - Eveleth; Virginia

were then most completely filled with pupils. final "age group" cycle in the mining towns will be characterized by an abnormally large adult population. Declining industry will cause youth to leave for fields of opportunity elsewhere. The old will remain behind with vested interests in the community. The Mesabi has not reached this stage fully as yet, but the relative number in the upper age groups as compared to the lower age groups has changed markedly in the last ten years as indicated in Table II. The group above 45 years of age was abnormally low in 1920 compared to the state, but in 1930 it was practically normal. The group under five years was low in 1930 compared to the state, and the group under 20 years of age was also low. The group 20 to 44 years was still high but not nearly as high as in 1920. These trends indicate that the range will soon have an abnormally large population in the upper age groups.

During the first period of the mining town's history births are few because of the disproportion of the sexes, and the sparsity of married couples. This period ends with the coming of prolific and youthful immigrant stocks which produces a high birth rate. Data on this point are incomplete but such as exist justify this summary statement. Hibbing's birth rate was about 45 per thousand for the period 1900 to 1909,[11] approximately 30 per thousand from 1920 to 1924, and about 22 per thousand from 1925 to 1929.[12] For the years 1928 and 1929 the rate was 20 which is about normal as compared to the United States registration area.[13] The rate for Virginia was very low for the first four years following the fire of 1900, but from 1905 to 1909 and 1915 to 1920 (data are not available for intervening years) was considerably above that of the United States registration area. Since 1920, Virginia's birth rate has fallen below the registration area. In 1929 it was only 15.6 per 1,000.[14]

Table II

Percentage of Population in Various Age Groups
for Hibbing and Virginia Compared to the State
of Minnesota, 1920 & 1930*

	Hibbing		Virginia		Minnesota	
Age	1920	1930	1920	1930	1920	1930
Years						
Under 20	43.5	42.4	38.0	40.2	40.4	44.5
Under 5	13.0	8.9	11.8	7.3	11.0	10.4
20 to 44	43.5	38.8	48.6	38.0	38.8	33.7
45 and above	13.0	18.9	13.4	21.7	20.8	21.8

*   Eveleth is omitted as it is under 10,000 population and, therefore, population is not analyzed for age groups in the U. S. Census.

The fluctuations in the death rate cannot be studied on the Mesabi because of a lack of complete data. Figures, available for Virginia for the years 1910 to 1927, and for Hibbing from 1918 to 1927, indicate that the rate has been considerably lower than for the United States registration area. This has been especially true since 1920 when deaths have been about eight per thousand in the range towns as compared to about 13 or 14 in the United States registration area.[15] Newspaper accounts make clear that the infant death rate was excessively high on the range during the two decades 1900 to 1920.

Violent deaths have also been high due to industrial hazards. Beyond this we can make no comments.

The bio-social cycles discussed are summarized in the next to the bottom part of Figure II. In this case the composite cycles in the three towns are illustrated, each line representing the origin, climax, and disappearance of the combined bio-social cycle of the three range towns.

Psycho-social Cycles

The matter of group attitudes over a period of history cannot well be measured statistically, yet newspaper accounts, and other local records, current group opinions readily expressed in interviews, as well as certain group activities, indicate quite as clearly the prevailing inter-group attitudes of a community. On the basis of such evidence the conclusions summarized below were reached, and are presented here without proof because of a lack of space.[16]

The first period was one of community integration. Laborers, industrialists, and public (groups represented in local government) in the range communities worked together in the face of common dangers and common hazards to maintain themselves and found their civilization. Forest fires,[17] severe winters, uncertainties in finding a market for the ore, and other similar circumstances kept the community integrated to an unusual degree. Soon after 1900, when the great corporations took over the mines, and when the towns were well founded an inter-group conflict cycle developed that reached its climax in about 1912 and continues unabated. This period ushered in periodic industrial conflicts, and more important still, perpetual public-mining company conflict. Mining company taxes were the chief issue of contention. The towns began a regime of spending that led the mining companies to institute lawsuits and various restraining actions against them and their building and recreation programs. Allegations of graft in public office became the order of the day in city government.[18] Politicians made the most of their office to reward their friends; patronage existed on every hand. The predatory pattern of the heartless and exploiting corporations became that of the local community also, and the mining companies were the victims of it. Besides paying large tax revenues the companies faced many damage suits in Hibbing which aimed at collecting damages for blasting near residences and at receiving remuneration for the deterioration of property values due to mining activities.

Each group has carried its issues into the state courts and into the state legislatures. Citizens' damage suits against the companies have been carried to the United States Supreme Court. Each group has tried to gain at the expense of the other. Up to 1920 the towns held the position of ascendancy and defied the mining companies successfully, but always with a narrow margin of power. Since that time the tide has turned and the mining companies are making the communities bow. The original death blow to town domination came in the per capita tax limitation law of 1921 which limited expenditures for municipal purposes to $100 per person. The law was amended in 1929 calling for further reductions annually until 1933 and thereafter when expenditures are limited to $70 per capita. There is considerable evidence that hereafter the mining companies will dictate local policies to a much greater degree.

Explanation of Figure II

The figure at the top in the form of a normal curve represents the growth, maturity and decline of the mining town civilization. The first period is the pioneer period which represents what Chapin has called the period of growth; the middle period of the mining civilization is one of conflict, which corresponds to Chapin's period of maturity; the final period on the Mesabi will be one of decay and disintegration. The mining towns will no doubt eventually be replaced by small agricultural trade centers.

The diagrams on the four levels below represent minor cycles of change. Each minor cycle is described as follows:

Culture Cycles

—— Life Evaluation Cycles (Mores)
    1. Life held cheap
    2 and 3. Well-developed protective culture

········· Moral Standards Cycles(Mores)
    1. Tolerance of vice
    2. Tolerance of paternalism and graft
    3. Economy mores in government

--- Material Culture Cycles
    1. Simple material culture
    2. Lavish material culture
    3. Decay of material culture

Psycho-social Cycles

—— Group Relations Cycles
    1. Integration
    2 and 3. Conflict

········· Dominance/Submission Cycles
    1. Public ascendancy
    2. Mining Co. ascendancy

--- Industrial Groups Cycles
    1. Individual capitalists
    2 and 3. Predatory corporations

Bio-social Cycles

—— Birth Rate Cycles
    1. Few married couple and few births
    2. High birth rate
    3. Low birth rate

········· Age Groups Cycles
    1. Young adult males
    2. Disproportionately large number of children
    3. Disproportionately large number of old people

--- Population Growth Cycles
    1. Boom growth
    2. Stable population
    3. Decline

---- Sex Ratio Cycles
    1 and 2. Males predominant
    3. Balanced

Physico-social Cycles

—— Geographical Resource Cycles
    1. Extent of ore unknown
    2. Abundant supply located
    3. Supplying rapidly diminishing

········· Social Policy Cycles
    1. Discovery and development
    2. Exploitation
    3. Conservation

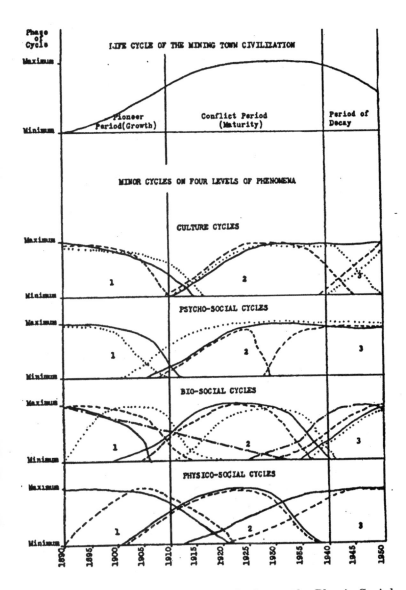

Fig. II. A Superimposition of Change Cycles on the Physio-Social,
          Bio-social, Psycho-social and Cultural Levels Indicating
          Their Synchronization on the Mesabi Iron Range.

The group factor and the dominant inter-group attitudes can be presented diagrammatically in a similar chart
to the foregoing indicating dates when the characteristic
psycho-social phenomena were most characteristic, so are
summarized in the middle section of Figure II.

Cultural Cycles

The mores. The municipal mores of the mining town
experience three distinct phases. First there is a period of
tolerance of vice prostitution, gambling, fighting, and drinking. This is clearly indicated in the papers of the nineties in
the Mesabi towns. Numerous accounts of drunken brawls,
deaths from exposure of homeless men in drunken stupors,
stabbing affrays, reports of the capture of escaped criminals
who had fled from other cities to the range towns to lose
their identity, raids on gambling devices by county officials,
cases of the passing of counterfeit money, of the printing
and forging of mining company and lumber company
checks, of the jumping of rooming-house board bills and of
hotel bills, of the operating of "blind pigs" to avoid the pay-
ment of the liquor license--all these appear as news items.
According to statements of early residents, prostitutes,
gamblers, and saloon keepers had a respectable status in
the communities. The prostitute walked the streets by day
without shame or disgrace and the saloon keeper's favor
was to be courted if one were in politics.

Before 1910 the purity leagues succeeded in changing the more on these points and the house of prostitution
sought the wilderness outside the towns or disappeared; the
saloons were regulated by state laws, and the gamblers
plied their trade in secret or moved on to new frontiers.

Public mores from 1910 to 1930 can best be characterized by the general concept of patronage plus many
in public spending; these were not only practiced but sanctioned by community mores. The patronage cycle is a phase
of the conflict pattern--the local communities have fought

the predatory corporations through preying upon tax revenues. The mores have sanctioned the predatory pattern as it is exercised by the communities. The people say, "Let's get all we can. If we don't get it, it will go to buy cigars for them damn capitalists down East."

As ore reserves decline undoubtedly the municipal mores will come to be characterized by economy to some degree. Perhaps this characteristic of the mores will lag far behind the need for it. At least this has been the case in Hibbing and Eveleth since the enactment of the per capita limitation law. Expenditures in Eveleth have each year run over the per capita limit, and injunctions against spending more have been imposed by the mining companies. Her obligations are about a year ahead of her income. The need exists for economy mores and some of the citizens want economy. Many of them, however, still want the spoils of political patronage.

Another field of the mores quite definitely marked is that involving the regard for life, or what might be termed the "protective complex" of the society. During the early days in the mining towns, life was cheap, partly from carelessness, partly from necessity. Natural catastrophe took a toll here where the sheltering influence of well-developed material culture did not exist; vice also took a high toll here where the mores did not protect a man against his lower appetites; suicide took a toll here where single men were detached from family and friends; industry took a toll, for basic needs called for practical rather than protective machinery. Naturally life came to be held cheap.

The suicide rate since 1900 is shown in Table III. to 1910 it was excessively high. It was probably much higher than these figures indicate as the State of Minnesota did not get into the United States registration area until that time. The cards reporting deaths indicate that a death was violent but frequently fail to indicate whether it was accidental, suicidal, or homicidal. The absence of suicide cases in Eveleth from 1901-1905 is probably due to poor reporting, for there were violent deaths during the period for which the method of commission is not indicated.

The fatality rate in the St. Louis County mines per 1000 workmen has been as follows:19

Period	Fatalities per 1000
1898-1905	5.93
1906-1910	4.82
1911-1915	2.64
1916-1920	2.52
1921-1925	2.05
1926-1930	1.81

Material culture cycles. Definite cycles in material culture can be observed and measured as well. The financial index is probably the most indicative of the state of material culture of a community. For the sake of brevity the per capita total tax levied in the three towns for all purposes (Table IV) and the per pupil value of all schoolhouses and sites (Table V) only are presented here. Each set of figures tells the same story,--a period of simple, crude material culture which ended before 1910, followed by a rapid flowering of material culture which probably reached its climax around 1930 (considering the existence of the per capita law). Soon decline will come with decreased revenues.

Cycles in material culture and in the mores are summarized diagrammatically in that part of Figure II labeled "culture cycles."

Summary

In the foregoing pages certain selected cycles have been presented to indicate the synchronous nature of periodic cycles on four levels of phenomena in the mining town.

Table III

Number of Suicides and Rates per 100,000 Summarized by
Five-Year Periods for the Three Range Towns* and for the
United States Registration Area *

Period	Hibbing		Eveleth		Virginia		U.S. Registration area
	No.	Rate	No.	Rate	No.	Rate	Rate
1901-1905	7	28.4	0	0	15	73.1***	13.9
1906-1910	11	27.8	7	22.0	6	13.8	16.0
1911-1915	5	9.3	5	14.1	11	19.1	16.3
1916-1920	3	4.3	1	2.8	8	12.0	12.3
1921-1925	9	11.8	6	16.5	12	17.9	12.1
1926-1930	14	18.0	9	24.2	15	23.9	13.2#
1901-1930	49	14.4	28	14.2	67	21.1	14.0

  *Data for Range towns were tabulated from the card files
   of the State Board of Health, St. Paul
 **United States rate is an average of annual rates.
     The average for Range towns is an actual average of
     periods as given based on estimated aggregate
     population and aggregate suicides for the respective
     periods.
***For 1902-1905 only. No records were kept for 1901.
     The fire probably led in part to the high rate.
     #1926-1928 only.

In the study of the Range it early became obvious
that there have been two rather distinct periods in its history. The pioneer period is clearly marked by certain definite
characteristics. Gradually this shifted to a period of extravagance which

Table IV
Per Pupil Value of Schoolhouses and Sites
1895-1930*

Year	Hibbing	Virginia	Eveleth
1905	$57.07	$97.94	$111.10
1910	177.67	15.77	113.13
1920	119.63	188.49	144.68
1925	603.40	395.87	257.35
1930	707.95	727.88	431.15

* Based on County Superintendent's annual reports to the
  State Superintendent of Public Instructions. All values
  are reduced to the 1910-1914 dollar values on the basis of
  the wholesale price index developed by the U. S.
  Department of Labor. Data are not available for 1915.

has persisted to the present time. During very recent years
evidence of decline is beginning to be observed, and certain
tendencies indicate that soon there will be a marked
decline. The pioneer period ended between 1905 and 1910.
This was followed by the period of extravagance. The period
of decay began only recently and decay may not become
characteristic for ten or fifteen years yet.

In order to make Figure II complete, then, this life
cycle has been presented in the form of a growth curve
similar to that in Chapin's theoretical graph, and this curve
has been superimposed on the time chart along with the
diagrams representing minor cycles of change.

Table V

Per Capita Total Taxes Levied, 1900-1930*

Year	Hibbing	Virginia	Eveleth
1900	$8.54	$2.87	$1.66
1905	22.72	2.65	10.74
1910	86.24	47.32	38.68
1915**	137.78	50.03	69.82
1920	134.73	48.30	121.61
1925	209.00	68.49	140.10
1930	219.64	92.05	173.40

* Based on State Auditor's Annual Reports. All values are reduced to the 1910-1914 dollar values on the basis of the wholesale price index developed by the U. S. Department of Labor.

** Figures approximate rather than exact as populations for these years are estimated.

The composite figure indicates that certain synchronous cycles mark fairly definitely the pioneer period of the mining town (Chapin's period of integration), other cycles mark the period of maturity, and certain trends that are now in the making indicate that still others will characterize the final period. The three historical phases of the life cycle are broken by the shifting minor cycles as nearly as historical trends are ever broken. Naturally the old gradually merges into the new. The dating of any historical event is to some extent arbitrary. The general period of origin and decline of a cycle can, nevertheless, be observed.

Synchronization does not necessarily mean causation. It may only indicate coincidence. However, if one examines the nature of the cycles on the various levels it becomes obvious that there is a causal relation between the cycles on the four levels and the total municipal civilization.

The characteristic civilization proves to be a composite of these influences as can be induced from the preceding discussion, and as might be much further elaborated if space permitted. There is an interrelation between the minor cycles on the different levels also. For instance, the social policy of exploitation grows out of the fact of the apparent inexhaustibleness of ore; the poorly developed protective mores are due to the emergencies of the frontier and to the predominance of the male sex in the population; the vice mores grow out of the uneven sex ratio also. Social integration is produced by the mutual struggle for maintenance which in turn is explained in part by the individual (rather than corporate as in the later period) nature of the mining enterprise.

The concurrent disappearance of a series of minor cycles and the initiation of new ones marks the beginning and end of periods in the total civilization of the mining towns. The period of maturity is not primarily a matter of a massing of a majority of cycles as suggested in Chapin's discussion, but in this case appears to be the product of minor cycles most of which are peculiar to the period. This superimposition suggests another interesting characteristic Minor cycles in those realms most remote from culture change first, while changes in culture itself lags behind. Change in the resource aspects for instance foreshadows an ultimate change in culture building trends. The change in the resource may not be reflected in culture until some years after it is obvious in the lower level. Abundance of ore followed by corporate management, followed by a public-mining company conflict will be followed by extravagance in culture. A period of delay between the appearance of the socio-geographical factor and its reflection in culture building seems natural when one stops to analyze it in a community which is so closely dependent upon a single resource.

By way of caution it should be stated that in this discussion no attempt has been made to analyze the influence of outside contemporary culture in stimulating or directing the changes that have occurred on the Mesabi. It must, of course, be recognized that underlying the exploitation of the ores of the Mesabi lay the demands of an iron age in the larger world outside. Likewise the machine culture dominating range civilization is a part of the American complex as are all phases of the culture. The problem has not been to emphasize this aspect, but rather to show how contemporary American culture as represented in the rather unique configuration of an iron range passes through its life cycle as a unique type of civilization.

The validity of Chapin's hypothesis is attested by the culture of the mining town, and it is clear that the periodic synchronous minor cycles not only characterize material and non-material culture, but also underlying levels of phenomena bearing directly upon cultural change in a given area.

Whether the life cycle theory is applicable to cultures universally is beyond the scope of this discussion. If it is applicable to cultures in general[20] one striking difference from the mining town cycle would probably be found. The time span of the culture would be much greater. The transitory nature of the mining town is too well known to justify proof. The mining town appears with the discovery and demand for the resource its area possesses. When the resource is gone it vanishes, leaving behind only the ghostlike shadow of its former prosperity. A civilization built on a soil resource, which is exhausted very slowly, might well have a life cycle spanning centuries.

Footnotes for chapter XV

1. Cultural Change, ch. 7. See also F. S. Chapin, "A Theory of Synchronous Culture Cycles," Social Forces, 3, 596-604; May, 1925. Briefly stated, Chapin's hypothesis is that a civilization has a life cycle induced by synchronous cycles of material and non- material culture change.

2. Especially noteworthy is the experience of the seven
   Merritt brothers who opened the first mines on the
   Mesabi, and began the building of the first railroad. See
   P.H. DeKruif, Seven Iron Men.

3. Biennial Report of the Minnesota Tax Commission, 1930,
   p. 19.

4. Ibid., 1928. Reprint p. 10. This figure includes the
   Vermilion and Mesabi Ranges together.

5. Minnesota Mining Directory, 1930.

6. Ibid.

7. Ibid.

8. Eng. and Ming. J. Jl. 17, 1926, p. 84; Ming. and
   Metalurgy, Aug. 1926, p. 339; Ibid., Jl. 1926, p. 281;
   Minnesota School of Mines Bul. No. 7.

   It is obvious that no prediction can be absolutely accu
   rate. The future demand for Mesabi ore will be condi
   tioned by the extent to which iron continues to be used in
   American culture and the degree to which new fields are
   exploited and their ores imported to the furnace centers
   by way of the St. Lawrence. The future of the range will
   also depend upon the degree to which low grade ores can
   be utilized at a profit, which in turn depends upon tax
   rates in Minnesota, transportation costs, mining costs,
   "beneficiating" costs, etc.

9. School data are used since the towns were too small to be
   analyzed into age groups in the U. S. Census in the early
   periods.

10. This trend is offset in part by changed educational
    mores for the upper age group, the building of local junior
    colleges, etc.

11. Table XVII, Third Biennial Report, Minn. State Board of Health, 1911.

12. Unpublished tabulations in the office of the State Board of Health in St. Paul. Available only for the years cited.

13. Annual Reports United States Census, Births, Stillbirths and Infant Mortality Statistics.

14. Op. cit.

15. Mortality Statistics, U. S. Census.

16. See full ms. for a complete summary of historical events.

17. Virginia was completely destroyed by a forest fire in 1893 and a large part of the business section was again destroyed in 1900 by a fire originating in a local saw-mill. All of the range towns were threatened again and again by forest fires.

18. This is not true of Virginia, probably due in part to the relatively larger part of taxes paid by local residents as compared to Hibbing and Eveleth.

19. Annual Report, St. Louis County Mine Inspector, 1905 to 1930. For previous years see Biennial Reports of Minnesota Department of Labor. Most of the Mesabi Range is located in St. Louis County.

20. Wissler suggests, "Tribal cultures have life cycles, like individuals of a species. They spring from parent cultures, grow, mature, beget other cultures, decline, and eventually die." Man and Culture, p. 212.

Chapter XVI

WHERE DOES THE DYNAMICS OF CULTURAL CHANGE RESIDE?

Cultural Change and Social Change as Distinct Processes

Studies in social or cultural change have so far not differentiated social and cultural change. In fact, the tendency seems to have been to consider social change and cultural change terms that may be used interchangeably. For the purpose of some studies a distinction may not be necessary since the social and cultural are vitally related. When one comes to locate the drive back of cultural change, however, a clear definition of these realms of phenomena seems desirable.

The social and the cultural are in reality distinct phenomena. Society is composed of interacting groups of individuals, whereas culture is composed of tools, methods, codes, and forms that the interacting groups produce and through which they function. A similar distinction may be made in discussing change. Social change would then be used to describe changes in society, and cultural change to describe changes in culture.

In this discussion, therefore, "cultural change" will be confined strictly to changes in the man-made tools, mores, and folkways. "Social change" will be used to describe changes in group composition (age, sex, vitality, mobility, etc.) and changes in the interaction processes (conflict, cooperation, domination, subordination, etc.) that characterize inter- and intra-group relations.

The distinction between the social and the cultural is recommended, especially in studies of social and cultural change in order that we may avoid the common error of attributing to culture forces which it does not possess. The use of such phrases as "culture is dynamic," "culture produces culture," "history repeats itself," unless they are carefully defined erroneously implies that culture has resident forces which in reality reside in the social group and not in culture. There may be no objection to the use of such phrases as long as they are confined to a purely descriptive meaning implying only that culture does change and is not, therefore, perpetually the same. They can, however, hardly be accepted when held to mean that there are forces resident in culture which produce change in culture. On the other hand, there seems to be no comparable objection to saying that "the group produces culture," "society is dynamic," "group experience determines culture trends."

An exact definition of cultural change and social change will differentiate them and in so doing will clear the ground for a more penetrating analysis of both social change and cultural change.

In this study of cultural changes in the mining towns on the Mesabi Iron Range in Minnesota it became apparent that the fundamental forces directing cultural change and shaping the culture pattern existed outside of culture although they were intimately related to it. They were for the most part social forces as above defined.

Relations of Group Interaction Pattern to the Culture Pattern

The pioneer period in the history of the mining towns was distinguished from later periods by definite social characteristics such as a predominantly large male population, a disproportionately large prostitute

class of women, a disproportionately large age group in the most energetic period of life. The mines were privately owned and were operated on a small amount of capital. Although everyone on the range depended upon the mines for a living, their success was uncertain. This situation produced a high degree of integration in the mining town society. Cooperation was necessary in order to assure maintenance and survival of the social group in the struggle with nature.

As soon as survival was assured, a more normal population group migrated to the area--women and children, married men, and business and professional classes. Great corporations, including the United States Steel Corporation, purchased the ore reserves. This constituted a change in the composition of the social groups. A change in the interaction pattern accompanied this change. Absentee ownership of the iron mines by corporations initiated an era of strikes on the part of the laboring group and of lawsuits between mining companies and the range towns. The societal interaction pattern thus became a conflict pattern.

It is these changes that have been designated "social changes," changes in group composition and in the dominant interaction patterns of the society. The term "culture change" is not at all applicable to them, although culture change proceeds along with these social changes and may be to a considerable extent induced by them.

Culture, on the other hand, during the pioneer period was very primitive. Folkways were realistic, and the mores tolerated many forms of behavior condemned in normal American communities. Mesabi Range pioneers lived near to nature, wresting a food supply largely from the native animal life and making shelters from logs and rough unplaned lumber taken from the native pine trees. The saloon keeper, the gambler, the prostitute, the escaped criminal and renegade from established towns beyond were all accepted as satisfactory citizens. Numbers were more important than quality in these-communities where forest fires, severe winters, and hard work called for courage and endurance rather than refinement.

As the society became more normal in group

composition, culture changed very markedly. Complete families in the towns soon reduced the prostitute to a shameful status; the gambler had to learn to ply his trade in secret or move on to a new frontier; the saloon keeper was forced to abide by the state law on closing hours. The coming of professional people, of conservative business men, along with the increase in complete families and children soon led to the abandonment of board sidewalks, muddy streets, mining shacks, and cheap frame school buildings and put in their place public works unrivaled by American communities of equal size. These changes in the mores and folkways and in the material culture of the towns have been called cultural changes.

Culture Change as the Product of Interaction

When social change and cultural change are differentiated it becomes obvious that the two processes are to be a considerable degree causally connected. The data accumulated in this study of mining towns indicate that social change is in most cases the forerunner of cultural change and frequently induces the cultural change. This may be illustrated by showing how the change in the culture pattern of the mining towns seem to have been brought about by a change in the dominant intergroup interaction pattern characterizing the society in two periods of its history.

During the pioneer period when integration characterized relations between the public, the mining companies and labor, the municipal culture pattern was marked by thrift, conservatism, economy, and simplicity. In the later period when the public and labor took a conflict attitude toward the mining companies, the municipal culture pattern became predatory in nature. Enormous sums of money were spent for public works, athletic programs and recreation.

The social interaction pattern characterized by group integration and solidarity of the first period was

causally connected in the case cited with the thrift pattern
in municipal culture. When life for all groups was a struggle
and when success was uncertain the matter of economy was
of common interest to the public, the laborer, and the indus-
trialist. Likewise in the second period there was a causal
connection between the conflict of groups and extravagance
in municipal culture. Extravagance in expenditure for public ornaments and public works was an expression of conflict between local residents and absentee corporation taxpayers. Thus in a very direct way change in the intergroup
relation (a social change) predicated a definite change in
the municipal culture pattern.

While a direct and causal connection between
change in a social interaction pattern and a culture pattern
exists, the analysis here has been oversimplified. To make
it more complete it must be pushed back to lower levels of
phenomena in the community.

The problem of change as it affects culture may be
attacked at four rather distinct levels. The first level, that
of changes in the physical environment, is basic, although
as such it is quite far removed from cultural change. The
physical environment undergoes two distinct types of
change from the viewpoint of causation. The one consists in
those changes that are initiated by forces inherent in
nature. These changes, with the exception of cataclysmic
changes, are orderly and recurrent, such as climactic and
seasonal changes. Culture is to a considerable degree
adjusted to these changes and tends to conform to them
from season to season. These adjustments come so automatically that they are seldom thought of as initiating forces in
cultural change.

On the frontier, however, men have to reckon with them in
making initial adjustments. The other type of change in the
natural environment is much more direct and consequential
to cultural change. It consists of those changes that grow
out of human activity in the environment. Such activities as
improving natural surroundings, harnessing sources

of power, discovering and using natural resources, all of which grow out of man's progressive adjustments to the natural setting, are typical of these changes.

Among the changes wrought in the physical environment by human activity on the Mesabi Iron Range have been the exhaustion of forests, the partial exhaustion of high-grade ores, the partial depletion of wild life, the clearing of lands and establishment of farms. These changes have reflected on societal activity and culture in many ways and have thus become determinants of other societal activities in the area. In this sense the tightening of the state industrial policy in relation to taxes and profits, the psychological outlook of labor as refers to security, tenure of position, and opportunity for work, the prospects of trade for business enterprises, these, and many similar changes may all be traced to diminishing resources in the natural environment wrought by the human impact upon it.

The second general level of change that bears on cultural change is the biological, that of changing population quality and numbers as these factors influence culture. This problem involves the question of relative mental capacity of different groups in the society, the problem of the sex ratio, and to some extent the distribution of social classes, and the density of population. Presumably all of these factors bear on cultural change, along with other variant characteristics of the human stock.

On the Mesabi Range, nationality groups have changed with the different waves of immigrants.Because of different experiences and capacities for adjustment, these peoples have played varying roles in the range communities. Nationality groups must be taken into account in interpreting birth and death rates, and also such cultural characteristics as are exhibited in fraternal, political, religious, and educational institutions.

Male-female ratio in the population, as well as other phases of the selective migration to the range during the period of its settlement was shown to have been important in shaping certain phases of the culture. Especially did the uneven sex ratio affect sex mores.

Changes in group composition and interaction constitute the third level of change. This aspect of change is exclusively in the social and sociological realm. Here is located the dynamic element in all cultural change, and the dynamic element for the second type of geographical change described, that of change in the environment through the agency of man, and also the force producing many of the changes just described.

Whether labor or capital, Protestant or Catholic, Democrat or Republican, industrial group or public plays the dominant role makes a difference in culture building. As control on the Mesabi Range shifted from one group to another, social organization was modified, and new cultural trends were initiated. The relationships existing between the groups in society started currents of interaction that had far-reaching import. Long prevailing interaction patterns in the group furnished the drive for consistent and long prevailing trends in culture building, as has been suggested in the preceding section.

It must be recognized that culture history is important to cultural change, as well as to geographical, biological, and social change. There is an intimate interrelation between all of these aspects of change. The natural and cultural environments are the milieu in which social interaction takes place. If man exhausts the soil or wastes the timber or ore, group interaction ceases because man abandons the area; if man modifies his customs, changes his laws, or perfects his tools, social interaction is modified by greater restrictions or greater freedom. Moreover, the cultural background provides the standards of value and the tools for the struggle for resources, and the culture defines the pattern for the struggle and sets its limits. With regard to migration to an area it may be said that the culture provides the standards of value which make certain resources of nature act as magnets drawing only certain population elements. The social group is the agent initiating change in the four realms described--geography, human biology, society, and culture--granting the exceptions noted.[1] Culture, like natural resources, and human capacity provide the conditions for social interaction.

Footnotes for chapter XVI

1. Changes in geography and biology that are wholly natural, and beyond human control.